D0708493

ARE YOU A
GRUMPY OLD GIT?
QUIZ BOOK

ARE YOU A
GRUMPY OLD GIT?
QUIZ BOOK

GEOFF TIBBALLS

Michael O'Mara Books Limited

First published in Great Britain in 2018 by
Michael O'Mara Books Limited
9 Lion Yard
Tremadoc Road
London SW4 7NQ

A CIP catalogue record for this book is available from the
British Library.

Papers used by Michael O'Mara Books Limited are natural,
recyclable products made from wood grown in sustainable forests.
The manufacturing processes conform to the environmental
regulations of the country of origin.

ISBN 978-1-78243-940-0 in hardback print format
ISBN 978-1-78929-082-0 in paperback print format
ISBN 978-1-78243-941-7 in ebook format

2 3 4 5 6 7 8 9 10
Designed and typeset by Design 23
Illustrations by Andrew Pinder

Printed and bound by CPI Group Ltd, Croydon CR0 4YY
www.mombooks.com

CONTENTS

INTRODUCTION

In recent years, scientists have made great strides in identifying some of the troubling conditions that afflict men of a certain age. They have studied genes linked to hair loss, forgetfulness, dad dancing and the urge to wear floral shirts but, perhaps most eagerly anticipated of all, they have finally managed to identify the holy grail of modern medicine – the grumpy gene.

For decades, experts have been puzzled by what causes many previously happy, carefree young men to become perpetual moaners as soon as they hit middle age. Suddenly their glass is not just half empty, it is drained to the very bottom; they worry that looking on the bright side will give them a headache; they are firmly anchored on cloud one. Male pattern grumpiness is a debilitating disorder that can result in prolonged distress and terminal boredom for anyone unfortunate enough to be within earshot. At first it was attributed to the pressure of raising a family or the realization that their wild youth was now just a distant memory, until a study of men who had been forced to go shopping with their partners instead of going to the pub revealed the presence of a specific grumpy gene. This expressed itself with seventy-nine per cent of those tested criticizing the ability of others to park a car, eighty-two per cent muttering about the intrusive elevator music, and ninety-one per cent insisting on telling complete strangers that they could remember when the shopping mall was 'all fields'. In further experiments, this gene was then isolated and injected into laboratory mice who immediately stopped running happily around their cages and instead started complaining about the price of cheese and how cats no longer showed them the respect they used to.

To discover whether you possess the grumpy gene, this quiz book has been devised to gauge your reaction to hundreds of different situations – from airport passport reader machines that spectacularly fail to work and dog walkers who never scoop the poop to parcel delivery men who choose to ignore the address clearly marked on the label and prefer to drop off your package at any random house in the neighbourhood. Never mind the correct number, the correct street and the correct town, you're lucky if they deliver it to the correct hemisphere!

Points are awarded for each answer, your total score indicating where you rate on the grumpy scale. You could then decide to take positive steps to lighten your general mood and spread joy to those around you or, of course, you could be perfectly content just to remain a grumpy old git.

ACCIDENTS

1. **While you are taking a shower your partner turns on the kitchen tap downstairs, causing you to be soaked in a sudden blast of ice cold water. Do you?**
   a) Say nothing.
   b) Mention it once in a jokingly accusatory tone and then forget about it.
   c) Bring up the traumatic incident for decades afterwards whenever the subject of conversation turns to showers, water, the cold, or near-death experiences.

2. **You accidentally bang your knee on the leg of a table. Do you?**
   a) Curse yourself for not looking where you were going.
   b) Curse the table leg for being in the wrong place at the wrong time.
   c) Angrily kick the table leg, thereby injuring your toe.

3. **You accidentally drop a coin down the tiny gap in the back of the sofa. Do you?**
   a) Leave it there because, in the great scheme of things, it's not a whole lot of money.
   b) Thrust your arm down into the gap as far as it will go, running the very real risk that your arm will become stuck and that you and the sofa will have to make an embarrassing trip to hospital in the back of an ambulance.
   c) Call on your neighbours and ask them to help you lift and tip the sofa upside down in the hope that the coin will fall out.
   d) Go to the shed, fetch a saw and proceed to hack the sofa into pieces, justifying your actions by saying: 'It's time we had a new sofa.'

4. **Have you ever looked for someone else to blame after accidentally biting your own tongue while eating?**

5. **You get a small splinter in your finger. Do you?**
   a) Try to extricate it yourself without making a fuss.
   b) Proffer the wounded digit to your partner with a pitiful, pleading expression in a manner reminiscent of Androcles and the lion.
   c) Call the emergency services, demanding that they come straight away and saying they may need to amputate.

6. **Your partner accidentally cuts her finger while she is a passenger in your brand-new car. Do you say?**
    a) 'Don't worry, darling. I'll pull over and fetch a plaster from the medical kit.'
    b) 'Don't bleed on the seats! Don't bleed on the seats!'

7. **If you drop something on the floor and fail in your first two attempts to pick it up, do you then make an angry lunge at it as if it was somehow the object's fault?**

8. **You fall over in the street after tripping on something and are instantly surrounded by half a dozen concerned passers-by. Your pride is more hurt than your body. Picking yourself up, do you say?**
    a) 'I'm okay, thanks. Don't let me hold you up.'
    b) 'What are you lot staring at? Haven't you got homes to go to?'

9. **Wearing only a pair of socks, you accidentally tread on a piece of your grandson's Lego. Do you?**
    a) Laugh it off and put the Lego brick back in its box.
    b) Issue your grandson with a list of health and safety instructions.
    c) Hobble around for the rest of the day, declaring to anyone who is listening that you could now be crippled for life.

10. Your partner inadvertently leaves a tissue in the pocket of a skirt that then goes in the washing machine and splatters your favourite dark shirt with tiny specks of white paper. On a scale of disasters, does this incident rank as more serious than . . . ?

a) The time *you* spilled red wine over *her* new dress.

b) Chernobyl.

11. Which of these is the most unlikely to happen?

a) You will be abducted by aliens while waiting in line at the Post Office.

b) You will be struck by a meteorite while sitting out in the garden.

c) You will be trampled underfoot by a herd of passing wildebeest while cleaning your car.

d) You will spontaneously combust.

e) Your insurance company will pay up on your accident cover without any quibble.

ANIMALS

1. **Early every morning for the past two weeks, you have discovered a pile of fresh dog poop outside your house. Do you?**
   a) Wearily put the poop in a bag and dispose of it in an appropriate manner.
   b) Mutter darkly that castration is too good for both the dog and its owner.
   c) Don balaclava and full camouflage gear and conduct a stakeout in the shrubbery all through the night, ready to pounce on the offending hound as soon as it assumes the squatting position.

2. **Do you consider squirrels to be?**
   a) Fascinating creatures that are a joy to have in the garden.
   b) Cute and cuddly.
   c) Vermin.

3. **If a black cat runs across the road in front of your car, do you think?**
   a) 'That's a sign of good luck for the day.'
   b) 'It's a shame I wasn't driving a bit faster.'

4. **If you had just witnessed Lassie run a mile to rescue a small boy from drowning in a raging torrent and had then seen her run another five miles to the nearest hospital to alert paramedics, would you have reported her anyway for being off the leash in a public place?**

5. **While visiting a friend's house, their cat jumps up onto your lap. Do you?**
   a) Stroke it.
   b) Ignore it.
   c) Snarl: 'Get it off me; it may have fleas!'

6. **Your young daughter's pet hamster accidentally gets sucked up the vacuum cleaner with fatal consequences. Do you?**
   a) Hastily replace it with a lookalike.
   b) Tell her: 'Fluffy went out to play in the garden and he decided to run off into the woods to lead a lovely, long, happy life roaming wherever he wants to. But before he went, he left you this goodbye note to thank you for being such a wonderful friend.'
   c) Tell her: 'The hamster got sucked up the vacuum cleaner. It's dead.'

7. **On a springtime family trip to the zoo, the animals in almost every enclosure you arrive at are mating. Do you tell your children?**
   a) 'They're only doing what comes naturally.'
   b) 'Don't look, and let's move along.'
   c) 'I'm going to write a letter of complaint to the zoo about this! It's disgraceful.'

8. **Which of these descriptions do you think best applies to cats?**
   a) Loveable and playful.
   b) Wonderfully independent.
   c) Insolent.

9. **An annoying bluebottle has been flying around the room. Do you?**
   a) Open a window and hope it flies out, in the meantime getting on with whatever you are doing.
   b) Armed with a rolled-up magazine, hunt it down with a vengeance, unable to proceed with your life until it has finally been splattered on the window pane, entrails oozing.

10. **When a puppy sits on your lap, does it always give you a warm feeling because?**
    a) It's so cute and adorable.
    b) It hasn't yet been house-trained.

11. **For the umpteenth time, a bird poops on your newly washed car. Do you resolve to?**
    a) Not get so worked up about it in future.
    b) Wash the car less frequently in future.
    c) Buy a shotgun.

12. **What is your view on wasps?**
    a) They are essentially harmless and won't sting you unless you provoke them.
    b) They are nasty bastards who, unlike bees, sting you for the sheer hell of it. The government should ban them from all picnic sites.

13. **Your partner wants to allow the cat to share the bed with both of you at night. Do you say?**
    a) 'Okay, if that's what you want, that's fine by me.'
    b) 'Maybe, but I'm scared I might roll over in my sleep and crush him.'

c) 'Sorry, you know I'm allergic to cat hair. I'll be sneezing all night.'

d) 'No way am I sleeping naked next to something with sharp claws, teeth, and a lifelong grudge against me.'

14. While you are out walking, a stranger's friendly dog jumps up at you and leaves muddy paw prints all over your jeans. Do you?

a) Brush it off and say it's of no consequence.

b) Mumble under your breath about the need to keep dogs under control.

c) Threaten to make the owner pay for the dry cleaning.

d) Threaten to report the animal to the authorities, even though it was only a Chihuahua.

15. Did you always feel that Flipper should have stuck to catching fish instead of showing off by solving crimes?

16. If you were an animal, would you be?

a) A rabbit – soft and cuddly.

b) A giraffe – tall and elegant.

c) A lion – handsome, proud and lets the females do all the work.

d) A porcupine – extremely prickly.

e) A dinosaur – not because you are powerful and imposing, but because you're an old fossil who is still living in the past.

BEHAVIOUR

1. **Which of the following have you done at one time or another?**
   a) Reprimanded someone else's child for laughing too loudly.
   b) Argued with an inanimate object.
   c) Extended a sulk into a second day.
   d) Lost your temper over a game of online Solitaire.
   e) Slammed down the handset on the phone so forcefully that you have broken it.

2. **If a fragrance were to be named after you, which of these do you think would best sum up your personality?**
   a) Compassion.
   b) Sensuality.
   c) Vigilante.

3. **If a neighbour called you an 'interfering old busybody', would you see it as a compliment?**

4. **Which of these appeals to you most nowadays?**
   a) A lively party with loud music.
   b) A dinner party with friends.
   c) A crossword puzzle and an early night.

5. **Do you only make new friends if one of your old friends falls out with you or dies, thereby operating a strict 'one in, one out' policy?**

6. **What is the best way for you to start your day?**
    a) A beautiful sunrise.
    b) A hearty breakfast.
    c) A smooth bowel movement.

7. **Is your motto in life: Let's get ready to grumble?**

8. **In attempting to extract a new manual toothbrush from its tightly sealed package, have you ever?**
    a) Broken a fingernail.
    b) Tried to lever the toothbrush out with a screwdriver.
    c) Stamped on it in the hope that the packaging will fall apart.
    d) Lost the will to live.

9. **When you turn back the clocks each year, would you ideally like to turn them back to the 1950s?**

10. **Does the sight of a newborn baby make you want to?**
    a) Cradle it in your arms.
    b) Hold its tiny hand.
    c) Throw up.

11. **Do family members now have to help you to the ends of sentences?**

12. **When you meet up with friends, what is the first thing you talk about?**
    a) Your partners.
    b) Your vacations.
    c) Your ailments.

13. **If you live in the northern hemisphere, do you start grumbling on 22 June each year that the days are starting to draw in?**

14. **Have any of the following ever told you that you have anger management issues?**
    a) Your best friend.
    b) Your bank manager.
    c) Your driving instructor.
    d) Your chiropodist.
    e) The minister at your wedding.
    f) The person giving you a job interview.
    g) Your yoga teacher.

15. **Are you looking forward to growing really old simply because it will give you the opportunity to shake your walking cane at people in a threatening manner?**

16. **How many drinks do you need before you can be persuaded to take to the dance floor?**
    a) None.
    b) A couple.
    c) Three or more.
    d) Wild horses could not drag you onto the dance floor.

17. Do you tell anecdotes that can go on for half an hour or longer?

18. How do you cope in a crisis?
   a) You are calm and rational, the voice of sanity and reason.
   b) You run around flapping like a headless chicken.
   c) You are usually the cause of any crisis.

19. In terms of martyrdom, could you give Joan of Arc a run for her money?

St Joan   St Olde Git

20. **Which of these are essential factors in your overall happiness?**
    a) A loving relationship.
    b) A healthy bank balance.
    c) A pair of shoes that don't pinch.
    d) Someone else's misfortune.
    e) You're never happy.

21. **Would you get the hump if your partner criticized you for trimming your toenails in bed?**

22. **Which of the following do you automatically mistrust?**
    a) Any cold caller at the door who begins their pitch with the words: 'I happen to be in the area.'
    b) Any cold caller at the door who begins their pitch with the words: 'I'm not trying to sell you anything.'
    c) Any cold caller at the door who begins their pitch with the words: 'Good morning, my friend, praise the Lord.'
    d) Anyone online who claims to be related to a Nigerian prince.
    e) Anyone with thin lips.
    f) Anyone with a beard.
    g) Any man wearing an excessive amount of gold jewellery.
    h) Any man wearing a ski mask and carrying a sawn-off shotgun.
    i) Anyone you don't know.
    j) Anyone you do know.

23. You put your glasses down somewhere but can't remember where. Do you?

a) Blame yourself for being so careless and forgetful.

b) Blame your partner for not knowing where you might have left them.

24. Do you regularly hunt high and low for your glasses, becoming increasingly irritated as the search goes on, only to find that they are on top of your head?

25. Would you struggle to be the life and soul of the party even if the party in question was a gathering of accountants and auditors?

26. Do most of your conversations now begin with a complaint about something?

27. Do you resort to wild exaggeration to justify your grumpiness? Have you ever used any of the following as excuses for making much ado about nothing?

a) Grumble: 'It's like walking through the foothills of Vesuvius' just because your next-door neighbour had a bonfire and a few scraps of charred material blew over into your garden.

b) Grumble: 'I'm not going out looking like a scarecrow' just because your partner has failed to press your trousers to your satisfaction.

c) Grumble: 'Are you trying to poison me or something?' just because the unopened packet of ham in the fridge is one day past its expiry date.

d) Grumble: 'I'd have been better off going to Sweeney Todd' just because your barber failed to trim your sprouting ear hairs.

e) Grumble: 'They use this street as a race track' just because a car goes along at one mile an hour over the speed limit.

f) Grumble: 'They're always away on vacation' just because your neighbours take a second short break in six months.

g) Grumble: 'All I ever seem to do is pay bills' just because two happen to arrive in the mail on the same day.

h) Grumble: 'I'll catch my death of cold in this house' just because your partner decides to open the window a crack to reduce the level of condensation.

i) Grumble: 'It's like an oven in here' just because your partner decides not to open the window.

j) Grumble: 'There's never anything decent in this paper, I don't know why we buy it' just because they still haven't published your letter to the editor.

k) Grumble: 'Why is nothing in this house ever where I left it?' just because you can't find your glasses case . . . again.

BOOKS

1. **When you read that Little Bo Peep had lost her sheep, did you think?**

   a) She was desperately unlucky.

   b) She was a little bit careless.

   c) She did it deliberately to claim on the insurance.

2. **After borrowing a book from a public library, have you ever complained to the library about any of the following?**

   a) A missing page.

   b) Handwritten notes in the margins.

   c) Corners of pages that have been folded over because the reader can't be bothered to use a bookmark.

   d) The remains of someone's breakfast on the pages.

   e) A spelling or grammatical error.

   f) An unsatisfactory ending.

3. **In the story of Goldilocks and the Three Bears, would you be the bear with the permanently sore head?**

4. **When Oliver Twist asked for more, did you think?**

   a) 'Poor boy, he needs a decent meal inside him.'

   b) 'I suppose there's no harm in asking, although the rules of the establishment were quite clear apropos portion control. The workhouse bosses were very much ahead of their time – after all, the childhood obesity crisis was only a hundred and seventy years around the corner.'

   c) 'Greedy little bastard.'

5. **Do you carry around with you a pocket book on English grammar so that you can quickly correct any errors made by family members, shopkeepers, visiting workmen or people on TV?**

6. **Do you think the *Harry Potter* books should be part of the education curriculum?**

   a) Yes, they have encouraged millions of youngsters to read books and feature characters that kids can relate to.

   b) No, it's not proper literature. They should stick with the classics like Shakespeare, Chaucer, Poe, Twain and Jackie Collins.

   c) Certainly not. If I had my way, Harry Potter would be burned at the stake for practising sorcery.

7. **In the tale of Little Red Riding Hood, who were you rooting for?**
   a) Little Red Riding Hood.
   b) The Wolf.

8. **Do you feel that, on his arrival in England from Peru, Paddington Bear should immediately have been repatriated as an illegal immigrant?**

9. **Which of these descriptions best fits Miss Havisham in Dickens' *Great Expectations*?**
   a) Tragic.
   b) Not very keen on housework.
   c) Wallowing in self-pity; she needs to get a grip on herself.

10. **Do you struggle to understand why Z-list celebrity first-time mothers always feel compelled to write a book about their experience, as if they were the first women in the world ever to have given birth? The Virgin Mary's baby book would have been worth reading, but that doesn't mean that every reality TV nonentity has to get in on the act.**

CHRISTMAS

1. **What is your favourite part of Christmas?**
    a) Buying presents.
    b) Opening presents.
    c) Sitting around the dinner table with all the family.
    d) Playing party games.
    e) When it's over.

2. **A group of young carol singers call at your door. Do you?**
    a) Give them some money and wish them a Happy Christmas.
    b) Hide behind the sofa and pretend you're not in.
    c) Go to the door and inform them that you'll give them some money when they learn to sing in tune.

3. **Your family comes to stay for Christmas, but your son-in-law unwittingly sits in your favourite fireside chair. Do you?**
    a) Keep your disappointment to yourself and sit somewhere else.
    b) Shoot him an evil glare in the hope that he will realize his mistake.
    c) Perch precariously on a high, backless stool,

announcing in tones of martyrdom: 'No, don't worry about me. I'll be fine here. I'm sure it won't make my lumbago flare up too badly.'

4. **In your eyes, who is the true hero of Christmas?**
   a) The Baby Jesus.
   b) Santa Claus.
   c) Rudolph the Red-Nosed Reindeer.
   d) Scrooge.

5. **If you had been the innkeeper at Bethlehem, how would you have dealt with the unexpected arrival of Joseph and the heavily pregnant Mary?**
   a) I would have found somewhere for them to stay.
   b) I would have told them they should have booked in advance because we always get busy at Christmas.

6. **Do you grumble that your grandchildren's new Christmas toys contain so much packaging that it fills the garbage bin to the very top, leaving no room for any other household waste for the next two weeks?**

7. **While wrapping Christmas presents, which of these occurrences are guaranteed *not* to put you in a festive mood?**
    a) Having to wrap something that is an awkward shape, like a bedside table lamp or a toy starfish.
    b) No matter which way you twist, turn or press it, there is not quite enough paper to wrap the final gift.
    c) As if attracted magnetically, the sticky tape sticks to the *outside* of the wrapping paper, removing the design and leaving Santa beardless in places.
    d) The sticky tape runs amok and gives you an unintentional eyebrow wax.
    e) The sticky tape splits on the reel, so that you lose the end of the tape and must dig your fingernail in to start again – a task every bit as complex and time-consuming as Fleming's discovery of penicillin.
    f) The new roll of wrapping paper keeps rolling up on itself, forcing you to employ every elbow and knee at your disposal to keep it in place. You suspect that the game of Twister was invented by someone who was wrapping Christmas gifts at the time.
    g) As well as cutting the wrapping paper, the scissors cut a hole in the tablecloth ... which was a gift from your partner's parents.

h) Your wrapping technique leaves so much to be desired that every gift looks like a heap of dough.

i) Someone says on Christmas Day: 'Who the hell wrapped this?'

8. **Have you ever refused to reward carol singers for 'just a few bars' and insisted that they perform a full thirty-minute concert before you part with a penny?**

9. **Your partner buys you a power drill for Christmas so that you can finally put up the shelves you have been promising for the past seven years. Do you say?**
   a) 'Thank you. That will be really useful.'
   b) 'Great! More damn work!'
   c) 'I asked for a case of wine and a Cameron Diaz calendar!'

10. **Have you ever complained to shop staff about Christmas displays appearing in August?**

11. **Does it irk you when you go to a restaurant in the middle of October and find that the Christmas menu is already operating? Who in their right mind would wish to extend the Brussels sprout-eating season that long?**

12. **When you look at all of the recent crossings-out in your address book before each Christmas, do you think?**
   a) 'It's sad that I've lost so many old friends this year.'
   b) 'At least I won't have to buy as many cards and stamps.'

13. Do you like to have a Christmas tree in your house?

    a) Yes, it brightens the room and makes everything feel joyful and festive.

    b) I'm not bothered either way, but I suppose a Christmas tree is traditional.

    c) No, I don't care how pretty a Christmas tree might look, I became fed up with finding pine needles all over the place. If they get inside your socks, they can leave you limping for days – you might as well scatter shards of broken glass across the carpet.

14. Do you insist on decorating the Christmas tree personally each year because, recalling the incident of the upside-down fairy, you don't trust others to carry out the task to your exacting standards?

15. Do you find wearing a colourful paper hat at Christmas to be . . .?

    a) Fun, capturing the true Christmas spirit.

    b) Demeaning, like dressing a dog in a waistcoat.

16. What do you disapprove of most about Santa?

    a) He represents commercialism at its most blatant.

    b) He encourages the growth of unkempt facial hair.

    c) He's too jolly.

17. For you, what best sums up Christmas?

    a) The season of goodwill – even to your neighbour who insists on slamming his car door at one o'clock in the morning.

b) Too much to eat.

c) Too much to drink.

d) Too expensive.

e) Too many relatives.

f) Leftover turkey on Boxing Day ... and nearly all the way up to New Year.

g) The same old Christmas songs.

h) Everyone sitting at different heights around the dinner table – one on a wicker chair so low he has to reach up blindly for his food, another on a stool so high he's in danger of suffering from vertigo, and a third with his torso squashed in a deckchair – all because you have more guests than dining chairs.

i) A cracker that, when pulled, goes off with such a loud bang that two elderly relatives think the house is coming under attack from a Panzer division.

j) Finding a cheap, useless prize in the aforementioned cracker. How many grown-ups really need a toy spinning top or a plastic mouse?

k) Playing charades with at least one person who doesn't understand the rules.

l) An uncle who barely drinks for the rest of the year but overindulges on free Christmas spirit and ends up falling asleep at the table with his head in the cranberry sauce.

m) Visiting friends or family and having to sleep either on a makeshift sofa bed that has an alarming tendency to fold in half while you are in it or in a bed designed for a six-year-old.

n) A shopping mall Santa wearing an ill-fitting red suit

and sneakers, who puffs on a cigarette and swigs from a can of strong cider as soon as the grotto is closed for lunch.

18. At the office Christmas party, do you usually?
   a) Relax and enjoy yourself.
   b) Pretend to relax and enjoy yourself while instead adopting the role of the responsible adult, which involves making a note of how much everyone is drinking and monitoring any behaviour that you deem inappropriate.
   c) Swerve the party altogether in favour of an evening at home in front of the TV.

19. Your works department is holding a formal Christmas dinner. Is your first thought?
   a) 'Oh, that will be fun.'
   b) 'How can I get out of it?' This is rarely an easy task since only a doctor's sick note, a pre-booked holiday (producing a receipt from before the announcement of the dinner date) or a death in the immediate family (cousins not allowed) are deemed permissible reasons for absence.

20. Your neighbour's house has a huge, illuminated Santa and reindeer on the roof. Do you think?
   a) 'It looks really bright and cheerful.'
   b) 'It looks really brash and tasteless.'
   c) 'I wouldn't want to have to pay their electricity bill.'

21. Receiving which of these would immediately spoil your Christmas?

a) A celebrity fitness DVD.

b) A pedometer.

c) Yet more socks.

d) A toupee.

e) A greetings card that leaves you covered in glitter and sparkle for the next three days so that you look like a Glam Rock star from the 1970s.

f) A book on improving your lovemaking technique.

g) An awful jumper from a relative who hasn't kept the receipt.

h) A pair of washing-up gloves.

i) A nasal strip to stop you snoring.

j) A book about a grumpy old git.

CLOTHES

1. **You find an odd sock. Do you?**
   a) Put it to one side, confident that its partner will turn up eventually.
   b) Think of it as a good reason for buying some new socks.
   c) Moan all day about the lost sock as if it were a missing pet.

2. **Your partner comes home with a new skirt that is slightly shorter than the ones she usually wears. Do you say?**
   a) 'You look great. It's lovely to see you showing off your legs.'
   b) 'You're almost wearing a skirt.'
   c) 'You look like mutton dressed as lamb.'

3. **You step in a piece of chewing gum on the sidewalk and it sticks to your shoe. How long does it take you to get over the distress?**
   a) Five minutes.
   b) One hour.
   c) The rest of the day.
   d) You never get over it, and devote every waking hour of the rest of your life to waging a one-man war against wantonly abandoned gum.

4. **Your partner suggests you buy a new sweater. Do you say?**
   a) 'Yes, that's a good idea. It's about time I updated my wardrobe.'
   b) 'There's plenty of life in my old one still. I like to get my wear out of it.'
   c) 'So now you don't like the way I dress?'

5. **Do you now think that golf sweaters are the height of fashion?**

6. **Do you think anyone wearing a leather jacket is . . .?**
   a) Stylish and cool.
   b) A motorcyclist.
   c) A troublemaker.

7. **Have you ever stormed out of a store in a huff because its widely advertised 'winter bargain sale' seemed to contain clothes only in sizes extra-small and extra-extra-extra-large, with nothing in between?**

8. **When you try on a pair of jeans that you have not worn for over six months, you discover that they are too tight around the waist. Do you?**
   a) Decide that this could be a good cue to lose a few pounds.
   b) Accuse the jeans of having mysteriously shrunk of their own accord while hanging up in your wardrobe.

9. **When buying a new jacket, what colour do you prefer?**
    a) Black.
    b) Brown.
    c) Stone.

10. **Have you reached the stage where you firmly believe that clothes exist for function, not fashion?**

11. **Do you believe that novelty carpet slippers bring footwear into disrepute?**

12. Do you think that ripped jeans are . . .?
   a) An interesting fashion statement.
   b) A complete waste of money. Who wants to pay a
      fortune for a pair of jeans with bloody great holes in
      the knees? In my day, you threw them out when they
      looked like that!

**13. Do you insist on wearing a collar and necktie every
   day – even if you are only driving to the local rubbish
   tip – and consider that any male not similarly attired is
   downright scruffy?**

**14. Have you ever calculated how much of your life you
   have wasted while struggling to open the wrapping
   on new shirts, with their endless pins, clips, pieces of
   plastic and strips of cardboard?**

**15. You see someone wearing a baseball cap back to front.
   Is the first word that enters your head?**
   a) Sporty.
   b) Trendy.
   c) Prat.

COMMUNICATION

1. **When phoning a customer helpline, how many times can you bear to hear an automated machine promise that 'your call is important to us' before your patience finally snaps?**
    a) One.
    b) Two.
    c) Three.
    d) Four or more.

2. **While waiting an eternity on a customer helpline to speak to what passes as a human being and listening to the same music over and over again, how regularly do you find yourself yelling at the automated machine?**
    a) Never – I am a model of patience.
    b) Hardly ever – I wouldn't waste my breath on them, and in any case, years of experience has taught me that my chances of a swift response from a real person are slim.
    c) Nearly every time – I just can't help myself.

3. **When the automated customer helpline machine at your internet provider helpfully suggests that you could save time by doing everything online, do you think?**

a) 'That's a good idea. Why didn't I think of that?'

b) 'The only reason I'm having to spend twenty-five minutes of my life that I'll never get back waiting to speak to someone from your blasted company is because I have no internet connection! That's why I'm calling you! Do you really think I would be doing this if there was an alternative? Do you think I woke up this morning and thought to myself: "What shall I do to make the most of today? Maybe go for a walk in the park? No, I know, I'll phone the internet company instead and spend the best part of half an hour listening to a bad instrumental version of Coldplay on a loop while waiting to be put through to the correct department. THAT'S SO MUCH MORE REWARDING."'

4. **As a general rule, do you think cold callers who phone your home during dinner about an accident that you haven't had should be?**

a) Retrained.

b) Disembowelled.

5. **A phone caller asks you to take part in market research and promises that it will only take two minutes. How long does it usually take in reality?**

a) Two minutes.

b) Five minutes.

c) Fifteen minutes.

d) You don't know, because you hung up the moment you heard the words 'market research'.

6. **You regularly receive phone calls from strangers thinking you are the local dentist, who has a similar number to yours. Do you?**

   a) Bark 'wrong number' and slam the phone down.

   b) Politely tell them they have called the wrong number.

   c) Tell them you can fit them in for an appointment at three o'clock on Thursday.

7. **Do you think emoticons are?**

   a) Fun.

   b) Pointless.

   c) The tool of the devil.

8. **On average, how long does it take you to write a three-line text?**

   a) Less than two minutes.

   b) About five minutes.

   c) Half a day.

9. **Have you ever refused to send a text because you were unable to punctuate it properly?**

10. **Do you think emails are?**

    a) Quick and convenient.

    b) Cold and impersonal. It's like proposing to someone by fax.

11. A friend sends you an electronic greetings card via email. Do you think?

a) 'That makes a nice change.'

b) 'Hmmph! That's not what I call a *proper* birthday card.'

12. You receive a letter out of the blue informing you that you have definitely won a prize – up to one million dollars! – in a nationwide draw that you have not even knowingly entered. Do you?

a) Start dreaming about what you might spend the prize money on.

b) Reckon cynically that you are more likely to win a ballpoint pen than a million dollars.

c) Rip up the letter and throw it in the garbage where it belongs with the rest of the junk mail.

13. Do novelty ringtones set your teeth on edge?

a) No, they brighten up my day and bring a smile to the face of everyone who hears them.

b) Yes, they're a damn nuisance. Nobody wants to hear the strains of 'Disco Duck' just as the coffin is being lowered into the ground.

14. Does it never cease to amaze you that every other day you receive a new charity envelope through your letterbox? How many old clothes do they think you have lying around waiting to be donated? Who do they think lives here – Madonna?

15. **Have you ever felt the urge to send a tweet?**
    a) Yes, I tweet regularly.
    b) Rather like eating crocodile meat, I've occasionally wondered what it would be like but I'm not brave enough to try it.
    c) Definitely not. If I want to keep in contact with someone, I'll pick up the phone. In any case, what do I want with followers? It sounds suspiciously like stalking to me.

16. **If you had to write a short tweet to describe your average day, which of these would be closest to the truth?**
    a) Got up. Went to work. Went out in evening for drinks and meal with friends.
    b) Got up. Went for long walk in the country, picnic lunch. Spent evening relaxing.
    c) Got up. Stayed at home all day, watching rubbish on TV. Went to bed. Another day ticked off.

17. **After sending an email, do you still mistrust the internet to such an extent that you phone the recipient anyway to make sure that it has arrived safely?**

18. **Someone is walking towards you in the street with their head down because they are busy texting. Do you?**
    a) Swerve around them to avoid a collision and continue on your way without passing comment.

b) Take evasive action and say: 'Excuse me, look where you're going.'

c) Plough straight into them to teach them a lesson – unless, of course, they're bigger than you.

19. Do you find it hard to have much confidence in the point being made by an opinionated contributor to an online newspaper comments section when he or she is unable to differentiate between 'their' and 'there'?

20. You book for a romantic weekend away in a country cottage, but on arrival you discover that you are unable to get a signal on your mobile phone. Do you?

a) Say there's nothing you can do about it and make the most of a weekend free from the stresses of modern technology.

b) Grumble endlessly about how ridiculous it is to have areas with no phone reception in this day and age.

c) Insist on climbing three hundred feet to the summit of a hill over two miles away just so that you can get a signal – even though there is nobody you need to call or are expecting a call from.

21. **Do you find it puzzling that many celebrities on Twitter appear to be under the illusion that the public is remotely interested in what they had for breakfast, what their favourite brand of air freshener is or in the fact that they are currently sitting in a taxi?**

22. **Your partner offers to buy you a smartphone as a present. Do you say?**
    a) 'Great. It will be really useful to have internet connection while I'm away from home.'
    b) 'Waste of money. All I want from a phone is the ability to make phone calls. What do I care what the weather's like in Buenos Aires or that the Bulgarian lev has fallen two points this morning?'

23. **Isn't it infuriating when you find an envelope which has such a meagre coating of glue that no matter how hard you lick, it flatly refuses to stick down?**

24. **Which of these statements apply to you?**
    a) I keep my mobile phone switched on at all times and carry it with me wherever I go.
    b) My mobile phone is usually switched on, except at night.
    c) I often forget to switch on my mobile phone, but it doesn't matter because I can go for months at a time without receiving a single text.
    d) I don't own a mobile phone.

25. Would you ever dream of posting endless pictures of your grandchildren on Facebook?

a) Yes, I'm proud of them and it's nice to share that with my friends.

b) No, it's a really tacky, smug thing to do.

c) What's Facebook?

EDUCATION

1. **Which of these grumbles about modern education do you agree with?**
   a) They should teach more of the traditional subjects at school. Every child should know the date when Christopher Columbus discovered America, even if, with hindsight, they think it was a bad idea.
   b) Why do they still bother teaching algebra? Since leaving school, I could count the number of times I've needed to know how to solve a simultaneous equation on the fingers of Captain Hook's left hand.
   c) School sports days have been wrecked by political correctness. Nowadays you can't have winners and losers, it has to be all about the taking part. If modern educators organized the Olympics they would simply give everyone a gold medal at the start and say: 'Don't bother racing each other. You've turned up. That's all that matters.'
   d) Why waste three years and a shedload of money studying for a university degree in stuff like the history of the bagpipes, beauty therapy, surfing or *Star Trek*? How many job opportunities are there where the successful candidate is Captain Kirk?
   e) All that university lecturers ever seem to want to do is go on protest marches.

f) The only thing that most students leave university well qualified for is binge-drinking.

g) Teachers were able to administer proper punishment in schools in our day. The cane, the leather strap, the slipper, the ruler, a blackboard rubber aimed at your head – yes, they really were the happiest days of our lives.

2. **At junior school parents' evening you are obliged to sit your ample backside onto an impossibly small classroom chair so that half of your butt is overhanging on either side. Do you?**

a) Put up with it and listen to the teacher's comments about your child as best as you can while silently praying that the chair doesn't suddenly buckle beneath the weight to leave you in an unsightly heap on the floor.

b) Choose to stand instead.

c) Demand an adult-sized chair, along with a cushion.

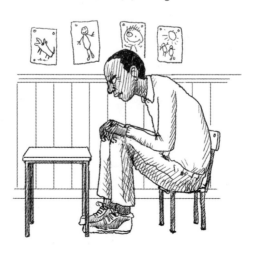

3. **Would you see a school reunion as an opportunity to . . .?**

   a) Meet up with old friends.

   b) Settle old scores.

4. **If you bumped into your old science teacher in the street, would you be . . .?**

   a) Pleased, and you would thank him for all he did for you at school.

   b) Dismissive, and you would relish the chance to tell him that you have succeeded in life in spite of him.

   c) Surprised, because he died ten years ago in an unfortunate incident with a Bunsen burner.

5. **When you see a line of huge, four-wheel-drive vehicles stopped directly outside the school gates at morning drop-off, do you think?**

   a) 'I suppose at least the parents are making sure the kids get to school safely.'

   b) 'When I was a lad, I had to walk to school – in all weathers.'

   c) 'Why do they have to drop their kids off so close to the school? Maybe if the kids had to walk more than a yard to the school gates, there wouldn't be an obesity crisis.'

FAMILY

1. **Your youngest daughter leaves home. Do you think?**
   a) 'I'll really miss her – the house will seem empty without her.'
   b) 'We might be able to rent out her room.'
   c) 'At last I'll be able to get in the bathroom in the morning.'

2. **Have you ever gone to bed early just because you were losing a family game of Trivial Pursuit?**

3. **Your daughter brings home a boyfriend who, in your view, supports the wrong football team. Is your subsequent attitude towards him?**
   a) Friendly in spite of his allegiance.
   b) Wary.
   c) Openly hostile.

4. **Your daughter brings home a boyfriend who has a large neck tattoo. Do you think?**
   a) 'I must get one of those. I'm sure it would create a talking point down at the golf club.'
   b) 'The only person who has ever looked good with a tattoo is Popeye.'
   c) 'Well, I wouldn't offer him a job if he turned up for an interview looking like that!'

5. You find a long hair on the soap. Do you?

a) Scoop it off and forget all about it.

b) Casually mention it in the expectation that someone will own up.

c) Send it off for DNA testing so that the family member responsible for the 'crime' can be identified and punished accordingly.

6. When your grandchildren start running around your lounge, what are you most worried about?

a) That they might hurt themselves.

b) That they might break something.

c) That they might get messy shoeprints on your new carpet.

7. Have you ever convened a full family meeting to determine who has been guilty of squeezing the toothpaste tube from the middle?

8. You learn that your new grandson is to be called Tyger. Do you say?

a) 'Very nice, very modern.'

b) 'What's wrong with "Norman"? It's a family name, you know.'

c) 'I suppose we should be grateful that at least it wasn't something like Heavenly Asteroid, Safari Picnic or Internal Combustion Engine.'

9. Have you ever needed to go for a lie down to calm your nerves after discovering that someone in the family has left the cap off the tube of toothpaste for the seventh time in the past fifteen days (according to the statistics displayed on your immaculately maintained wall chart)?

10. Practical jokes used to be such fun when you were a child, but now that you are a grandfather they somehow seem more threatening and humiliating. At which of these pranks by your grandchildren would you draw the line?
    a) Making rabbit ears behind your head in a family photo.
    b) Taping you into your favourite chair.
    c) Adding laxative to your coffee.
    d) Throwing a grape or a peanut into your open mouth while you are fast asleep.
    e) Pretending there's a spider on your shoulder when they know you're an arachnophobic with a dodgy heart.
    f) Phoning you at the restaurant to tell you that your house is on fire.
    g) Hiding your inhaler.
    h) Locking you in the cellar for six months.

11. Which adjective would best describe your mood on finding dried toothpaste in the sink?
    a) Indifferent.
    b) Disgusted.
    c) Vengeful.

12. **When your children lived at home, which of these used to drive you up the wall?**

   a) Doors being left open.

   b) Lights being left on when there was nobody in the room.

   c) People not turning off the bathroom taps properly at night, leaving them to drip, drip, drip, until you were forced to get out of bed in order to stop the sensation of Chinese water torture.

   d) People spending ages – and your money – making a call on the landline phone.

   e) Nobody apart from you ever bothering to take out the kitchen garbage bag, even when it was full to bursting point.

   f) People leaving so many hairs in the bath that there were enough gathered around the plughole to make a small bird's nest.

   g) People staying out late at night but forgetting their key, forcing you to get out of bed and answer the door in the early hours.

   h) Everyone suddenly dashing out when you would have welcomed help with cleaning the car.

   i) Being used as a free, twenty-four-hours-a-day, seven-days-a-week taxi service.

13. **Your daughter is getting married. Do you?**

   a) Tell her you'll support her every step of the way, credit card at the ready, to ensure her wedding day is the happiest day of her life.

b) Tell her to keep it cheap, because the more expensive the wedding, the quicker the divorce.

c) Skip the wedding altogether because it clashes with the first day of the football season.

14. **Do you still feel it necessary to remind some members of your family that the following do not grow on trees?**
    a) Money.
    b) New clothes.
    c) Toys.
    d) Cookies.
    e) Fruit.

FOOD AND DRINK

1. **How many times have you sent food back in a restaurant in the past twelve months?**
    a) Never.
    b) Once or twice.
    c) Three times or more.

2. **You are dining out at a restaurant, but the waiter forgets to bring your complimentary bread. Do you?**
    a) Discreetly try to catch his attention the next time he passes by way of a series of vague mimes and silent mouthing.
    b) Clap your hands and yell: 'Hey, waiter! Get your fat butt over here!'
    c) March into the kitchen and fetch it yourself.

3. **A friend brings some homemade parsnip wine for you to taste. It is vile. Do you say?**
    a) 'Yes, very nice,' and then make an excuse to rush to the kitchen to spit it out.
    b) 'Mmmm, it's certainly different, perhaps unique. I'm getting radiator fluid with a hint of rusty bolts and a bouquet of rotting badger.'
    c) 'I'd love a bottle – to clean my paintbrushes in.'

4. **A woman at the next restaurant table to you is very loud. Do you?**

   a) Try to ignore her.

   b) Pointedly move your seat a little further away from her.

   c) Join in her conversation uninvited.

5. **When you eat out, do you always go to the same restaurant and order the same things off the menu – and complain bitterly if your favourite dish is not available for some reason?**

6. **When you open the wrapper on a chocolate bar snack, is your first thought?**

   a) 'Hmm, I love chocolate. It's one of my guilty pleasures and makes me feel good about life.'

   b) 'Hmm, I'm sure these bars used to be a lot bigger thirty years ago.'

7. **Have you ever considered compiling a spreadsheet detailing instances where you feel that your partner's cooking has dropped below the required standard?**

8. **Is your favourite party tipple?**
    a) Beer.
    b) Wines and spirits.
    c) A soft drink.
    d) A nice cup of tea.

9. **When taking your grandchildren to a fast food restaurant, you study the illuminated screen menu (provided you have remembered your glasses) and decide that the BiffoMcWhoppery-GiantBurgery-BunFest is the most sensible item you can order in terms of damage limitation. Do you?**
   a) Announce your order confidently and clearly, as per the words on the screen.
   b) Mutter the order, hoping that no one else will be able to detect your embarrassment at having to spout such gibberish.
   c) Ask for the third item down.

10. **Which of these are hard for you to stomach?**
    a) Crumbs left in the butter container after someone else in the house has made toast.
    b) Peanut butter in the butter container because the same knife has been used for spreading both.
    c) Gravy that has the texture of water.
    d) A rogue fork in the knife drawer.
    e) A steak that is so rare you suspect a decent vet could get it back on its feet again.
    f) The juice of a fresh grapefruit that always seems to squirt into your eye with unerring accuracy.
    g) Sausages that are jet black on one side and as pink as a newborn piglet on the other. They're supposed to be turned, you know.
    h) An inefficiently loaded dishwasher.
    i) A satsuma or tangerine with more than two pips in each segment.

j) A slice of bread that gets stuck in the toaster, thereby forcing you to risk electrocuting yourself in order to rescue it.

k) A slice of toast that is browning slowly and gently under the grill until you turn your back for one second and suddenly find it is burnt to a cinder.

l) Ketchup bottles where most of the contents are encrusted around the lid.

m) Tomatoes that always manage to squirt on a clean shirt.

n) A toasted cheese sandwich where the corners of the bread are left bare.

o) Promisingly large bags of potato snacks that turn out to contain five per cent potato snack and ninety-five per cent air.

p) Tomato soup that splatters everywhere as it comes to the boil, leaving the kitchen looking like a crime scene.

q) People who leave their pizza crusts.

11. **You discover that the restaurant table at which you and your partner are seated is wobbly. Do you?**
   a) Grin and bear it.
   b) Ask to be moved to another table.
   c) Say nothing to the restaurant staff, but grumble to your partner about it throughout the meal.
   d) Order your partner to put her foot under the wobbly table leg.

12. **You have devoted what seems like most of a day to opening a can of salmon for lunch, yet no matter how many times you try, the can opener will not pierce the entire circumference of the obstinate metal lid. Do you?**

    a) Try and carefully prise the lid open with a knife or fork.

    b) In your frustration grab the sharp lid with your hand, cut yourself and bleed all over the salmon.

    c) Consider opening it with explosives.

    d) Decide to have ham instead.

13. **Do you resent the fact that when you were young you could eat whatever you liked without putting on a single pound but nowadays you can't take a bite of chocolate without feeling the need to rush to the bathroom scales?**

14. **Your daughter, who has recently become a vegetarian, comes to your house for dinner and your wife suggests serving a vegetarian meal to make her feel comfortable. You are a committed carnivore, so do you?**

    a) Happily eat the vegetarian food, knowing that it is only a one-off and that normal service will be resumed tomorrow.

    b) Moan throughout, saying that what this dish needs is a tasty pork chop on top.

15. **When eating out in a restaurant with a group of friends, do you make a careful written note of what everyone has ordered and also carry a pocket calculator so that you can make sure you don't pay a penny more than your share of the bill?**

16. **What are your feelings about locally sourced meat?**
    a) 'I think it's important to know where my food has come from.'
    b) 'All it means is that the restaurant has bought it from a butcher's shop around the corner.'
    c) 'I'm not interested in its name, its back story, its hobbies or its family tree; I just want it to taste good. I don't care if it was called Daisy and it lived six miles away on a seventy-acre farm overlooking a verdant valley, it won't stop me believing that its ultimate purpose in life was to be served medium-rare in a béarnaise sauce.'

17. **Have you ever moaned at a fast food restaurant because the supposedly 'regular' Coke is the size of a small vat? Regular for whom? King Kong?**

18. **It is unclear whether or not the service charge is included in your final restaurant bill. Since the service was perfectly satisfactory, do you?**
    a) Ask whether or not a charge has already been added on.
    b) Leave a modest tip anyway.
    c) Leave no tip on the grounds that if they don't make the terms and conditions clear, they don't deserve one –

but leg it to the door as fast as you can just in case an angry chef emerges from the kitchen wielding a meat cleaver.

19. **Have you become such an adept moaner that you can make finding a small bruise on an apple sound as catastrophic as a plague of locusts?**

20. **Do you think that drinking beer straight from the bottle is . . .?**
    a) Natural.
    b) Unhygienic.
    c) Coarse.
    d) For young people only.

21. **Does steam rise from your ears when you come across pretentious descriptions on wine bottle labels? Who in their right mind describes a wine as 'approachable'? So, what makes for an *unapproachable* bottle of wine – one that hides at the back of the supermarket shelf as soon as you go near it?**

22. **You stay at a small hotel where, instead of your usual cooked breakfast, the only option available is muesli. Do you say?**
    a) 'That will be much healthier for me than bacon and sausage.'
    b) 'What's this? Do I look like a gerbil?'

23. Which of the following have you ever grumbled about in a restaurant?

a) The restaurant is too quiet.

b) The restaurant is too noisy.

c) The restaurant is too dark.

d) The restaurant is too bright.

e) The print on the menu is too small.

f) Food that is served on a slate instead of a plate so that your boiled potatoes roll across the table and the sauce ends up in your lap.

g) Unsupervised children running around.

h) Pretentious terms on the menu – why does it have to be described as a 'jus' when we all know it's basically gravy? And what in God's name are 'artisan bread' and 'massaged kale'?

i) The service is too quick.

j) The service is too slow.

k) An accordionist who turns up uninvited at your table clutching a handful of wilting red roses that he'd just bought from the local gas station.

l) Being asked whether everything is all right by the staff more than once during each course.

m) The portions are too small.

n) The portions are too big.

24. What do you think is the best thing about having bran for breakfast?

a) It keeps your bowel movements soft and regular.

b) It is unique in tasting the same as the cardboard box in which it is packed.

c) You can drop it on the kitchen floor, accidentally tread on it in your carpet slippers, the dog can lick it, and it will *still* taste as good as new.

GARDENING

1. **On a particularly windy day, all the litter from your neighbours' bins blows down the street and settles in your front garden. Do you?**
    a) Uncomplainingly pick it all up and put it in your own bin.
    b) Pick it all up and scatter it in your neighbours' gardens.
    c) Take out a full-page advert in the local newspaper, naming and shaming the culprits.

2. **You discover to your dismay that slugs or snails have eaten your prized plants. Do you?**
    a) Accept that it is simply nature's way.
    b) Think about setting a beer trap for the murdering molluscs – until you realize it would be a waste of good beer.
    c) Pour salt on any slug you find and watch as its body bursts open from a surfeit of sodium chloride. Smile contentedly in the knowledge that if salt is bad for your health, it is even worse for a slug's.
    d) Fetch the biggest spade you can find, wield it like a club and set off in pursuit of anything with a shell.

3. **Has anyone ever suggested that you would be able to sharpen a pair of garden shears on the edge of your tongue?**

4. **Your partner kindly offers to do some weeding in the garden, but accidentally pulls up a seedling that you have been carefully cultivating for months. Do you?**
   a) Blame yourself for not telling her about the seedling beforehand.
   b) Blame her for not asking you whether there might be a valuable seedling somewhere in the garden masquerading as a weed?
   c) Ban her from the garden for life – except for hanging out the washing.

5. **Do you bristle when door-to-door garden care businesses want to charge you the earth just for sprinkling a few handfuls of fertilizer on your lawn? Perhaps they can plant a money tree while they're at it!**

6. **A small tree branch from your next door neighbour's garden has grown in such a way that it extends by a couple of feet onto your property. Do you?**
   a) Ignore it.
   b) Ask your neighbours whether they would mind if you cut back the branch.
   c) Sneak out in the dead of night and cut it back.
   d) Threaten to call the police unless the offending branch is removed within seven working days.

7. **Have you ever loved your lawnmower more than your family?**

8. **Have you ever installed any of the following to protect your garden shed in case anyone tries to steal your lawnmower?**
   a) An alarm.
   b) Security cameras.
   c) Searchlights.
   d) Barbed wire.
   e) Guard dogs.
   f) A leopard.

9. **Have you ever lain awake at night pondering why you keep finding discarded cigarette butts on your front garden when nobody in your family smokes?**

10. **Does seeing a garden crammed with ornamental ceramic gnomes make you want to . . .?**
    a) Smile.
    b) Sneer.
    c) Search for a large hammer.

11. **When children visit, have you ever posted either of these signs on your lawn?**
    a) No Ball Games.
    b) Keep Off the Grass.

THE GOOD OLD DAYS

1. **Do you find that, as the years roll by, you start an increasing number of sentences with the words 'In my day'?**

2. **On your annual reunion with the vacuum cleaner, a piece of it suddenly snaps off. Do you?**
   a) Blame your own clumsiness for the breakage.
   b) Grumble to your partner that they don't make household appliances like they used to.

3. **In your opinion, which of these aren't as good as they used to be?**
   a) Children's toys.
   b) The weather.
   c) The police service.
   d) Flavours of sweets and candies.
   e) Hairstyles.
   f) People's manners and common courtesy.
   g) TV presenters.
   h) Socks – most new socks you buy nowadays are so thin you could strain prunes through them.
   i) Sex.
   j) Public transport.

k) Sex on public transport.

l) Popular music.

m) A trip to the seaside.

n) Electric shavers – they used to be built to last, not to be replaced every couple of years. No wonder you see so many young men with big, bushy Victorian beards that look as if they might contain a nest of swallows.

o) Schools.

p) The postal service.

q) Lunch hours at work – nowadays you just about have time to eat a sandwich at your desk.

r) Teenagers.

s) Bending down and getting back up again.

t) Banks.

u) Hollywood blockbusters.

v) The length of time you have to wait to see a doctor.

w) Ring-pulls on cans – they're like death traps these days; one false move and you could easily lose a finger.

x) TV sets – you used to be able to play with the horizontal or vertical hold buttons to restore your picture; now you have to buy a new TV.

y) Nostalgia.

4. **Even though your fingertips were often left covered in ink after use and handwritten letters were sometimes little more than a series of connected smudges, do you still mourn the passing of the elegant fountain pen and its replacement in everyday life by the cheap and vulgar ballpoint?**

5. **Do you think the world has become a poorer place since so many households replaced the trusty old hot water bottle with an electric blanket?**

6. **And do you wish we still had eiderdowns instead of duvets 'because you can't trust anything that has a French name'?**

7. **Do you still refer to the post-war years of food rationing, lung-choking smogs and head lice as 'the good old days'?**

HEALTH

1. **Which of the following is likely to cause your face
    to turn beetroot red, your jaw to clench tight, your
    forehead to throb violently, and your blood pressure to
    skyrocket?**

    a) The morning mail delivery arriving midway through
       the afternoon.

    b) An apostrophe in the wrong place.

    c) Finding that the shirt you were going to wear on an
       evening out has a hole in it.

    d) Discovering that you have been short-changed.

    e) Sitting through an entire lunch with an attractive
       female client unaware that you had spinach in your
       teeth and a visibly long hair protruding from your left
       nostril.

    f) Finding that the CD rack has been tampered with
       so that your album collection is no longer in perfect
       alphabetical order.

    g) Discovering that a repair that you thought was insured
       under a household policy turns out not to be covered
       after all when you pore through the small print.

    h) Wilful shoelace knots that refuse to untie when you
       arrive home and are in a hurry to get your shoes off so
       that you can go to the toilet.

    i) A pencil whose lead repeatedly breaks.

j) The idiot who shouts 'in the hole' whenever golf is shown on TV.

k) The taxicab fare meter going up while you are stationary for eight minutes stuck in a traffic jam.

l) Noticing that someone has put the new toilet roll on the holder the wrong way round.

m) Discovering a worm cast in the middle of your immaculately mown lawn.

n) Hearing someone describe a smaller number of something as 'less than' instead of 'fewer than'.

o) People reading over your shoulder.

p) An incorrectly folded map.

q) A ballpoint pen that decides to run out of ink while you are halfway through writing down an important phone number from memory.

r) Holding the door open for someone who then fails to thank you for your courtesy.

s) Finding that the TV show you've been eagerly anticipating all week is a repeat.

t) Habitual sniffers.

u) Discovering that the perforations on the roll of double toilet paper aren't aligned.

v) Someone who, at the last second, jumps into your section on a revolving door as it swings around, thereby causing a collision and slowing down the entire revolution.

w) Sales assistants who give you your change on top of a receipt. Are they expecting a tip for facilitating the purchase of a tube of haemorrhoid cream?

x) Someone who replies to your valid point with 'whatever'.

y) Being mistaken for Nigel Farage.

2. **You get a small paper cut on your finger. Do you feel that it warrants the same level of sympathy that your youngest daughter received when she broke her leg as a toddler?**

    a) Yes – a paper cut hurts a lot. Unless you've had one, you don't know the pain and suffering it causes.

    b) No, definitely not.

3. **If you were granted a superpower, what would you choose?**

    a) The ability to fly.

    b) The ability to be invisible for a day.

    c) The ability to get the newspaper delivery boy to push your daily paper through your mailbox without shredding the back page so that it looks like a beginner's attempt at origami.

4. **Do you think a gym is . . .?**

    a) A good way to improve your fitness and overall health.

    b) A good way to catch other people's germs.

5. **Do you check your will at the start of each winter, just to be on the safe side?**

6. **What do you find most irritating about joggers?**

    a) The fact that they demand that you get out of their way so they won't have to break stride.

    b) The fact that they're so desperate to show they lead a healthy lifestyle and put you to shame.

c) The fact that they always look as if they're about to die at your feet, leaving you the bother of having to call a paramedic.

7. **You go down with a cold. Do you think?**
   a) 'It's only a cold. It will be over in a few days.'
   b) 'I hate colds. They really drag me down.'
   c) 'I'm gonna die, I'm gonna die!'

8. **You have been Googling your symptoms for more than four hours. Do you only stop when . . .?**
   a) Your fingertips start to bleed from incessant, frantic keyboard use.
   b) It is time for bed.
   c) The rest of the party guests have gone home.
   d) You finally find a disease you like, one which, while not life threatening, is impressive enough to elicit sympathy from others.

e) You find that the condition you are suffering from is called Obsessive Googling of Symptoms.

9. **Do you think that one of the best things about the internet is that it allows you to indulge your inner hypochondriac?**

10. **Your dental hygienist tells you off for not cleaning your teeth properly because areas of plaque have formed over the past six months. Do you think?**
    a) 'I'll make sure to follow her advice and brush better in future.'
    b) 'Why is she treating me like a child? I'm fifty-eight years old and a company director with awards to my name!'
    c) 'For the amount she charges, the least she can do is remove a bit of plaque. Otherwise I'm paying her just for doing a quick polish and telling me how well her eldest daughter is doing at university.'

11. **You fall over for the first time since you were a toddler, but because you are now sensitive about your advanced age, do you bridle when instead of telling friends that you 'fell over' the other day, your partner says that you 'had a fall'? You know that if, by some misfortune, you were ever to fall over again, friends would subsequently be told that you'd had 'one of your falls', making it just a short step before she feels the kindest thing would be to have you quietly put down.**

12. **If you get cramp in bed in the middle of the night, do you?**
    a) Try and work it off without getting out of bed and disturbing your partner.
    b) Gently climb out of bed and rub the affected area, hoping not to disturb your partner.
    c) Leap out of bed like Bob Beamon, with no concern about wrecking your partner's night's sleep, because all that matters at that moment in time is your own personal pain.

13. **When an old friend dies just before what would have been his eightieth birthday, are you particularly sad because ...?**
    a) He didn't quite make it to the grand age of eighty.
    b) You'd already bought his present.

14. **Do you refuse to use an electric toothbrush in case you receive a potentially fatal shock every time you put it in your mouth?**

15. **You suffer a persistent bout of hiccups. Do you?**
    a) Remain calm, certain that they will go in their own good time.
    b) Hold your breath for so long in an attempt to get rid of them that your face looks as if it is about to burst.
    c) Become increasingly frustrated and aerated as your hiccups refuse to disappear, leading you to fear that

you will end up like Charles Osborne, the American guy who had hiccups for sixty-eight years. You drink gallons of water and, when that fails, you resort to desperate and violent methods to shock yourself, although, at your age, stepping on the bathroom scales usually produces the same effect.

16. If an elderly lady suddenly collapsed in the supermarket, would you?

a) Rush to administer first aid.

b) Summon help from a member of staff.

c) Step over her because she was blocking the aisle.

17. **When you attend a funeral, do you usually take . . .?**
    a) Flowers, to pay your respects to the deceased.
    b) A large bag to take home as much free food from the wake as you can.

18. **Have you ever played ailment trumps where you attempt to earn sympathy by trumping someone else's medical condition with a more serious one of your own? 'I'll raise your bad back, high blood pressure and gout with a bad back, high blood pressure, gout and a gastric ulcer.'**

19. **When you read about people wailing that their non-essential cosmetic surgery procedure went wrong, leaving them with a facial expression that is unable to register the difference between surprise and anger and the sort of lips more usually seen attached to a fishing hook, do you feel even the slightest bit of sympathy for their plight?**

20. **Of which of these are you intolerant?**
    a) Wheat.
    b) Lactose.
    c) Gluten.
    d) People who cough in health centre waiting rooms.
    e) Rude doctors' receptionists.
    f) Nosey doctors' receptionists.
    g) Doctors' receptionists who are too busy filing their nails to deal with your emergency bout of man flu.

h) Patients who think it's all harmless fun when their children start hurling pieces of Lego around the health centre waiting room.

i) Medical staff who have eaten garlic the night before.

j) The anaesthetist telling you before your operation that you're so overweight he may have to use a tranquillizer dart.

k) Nurses who tell you the needle will be 'just a little scratch' but leave your arm looking like you've recently been wrestling a chainsaw.

l) Doctors who make you an appointment for eight-thirty in the morning but then roll in half an hour later without a word of apology.

m) Doctors who practise their golf swing while you are explaining your symptoms.

n) Doctors who gabble through their diagnosis, using long medical terms and are then irritated when you ask them to explain it again in words you can understand.

o) Adult acne – not having unsightly spots ought to be one of the few benefits of growing old.

p) People who sneeze over-dramatically – often with an accompanying exaggerated body jerk. For God's sake, it's a natural bodily function; you're not trying to win an Academy Award.

q) A thwarted sneeze. You're all prepared, paper tissue in hand, but nothing happens. However, you know that a full-blooded sneeze is imminent and is waiting to be unleashed at the most embarrassing moment, just as you have a mouth full of sausage roll at an important social function.

r) Dentists who charge exorbitant fees that rise at ten times the rate of inflation and then tell you all about the Caribbean cruise, the African safari and the two city breaks they have been on in the past six months.

s) Dentists who expect you to conduct a conversation with them even though they have forced your mouth wide open and have filled it with suction tubes and chunks of cotton wool.

HOBBIES AND RECREATION

1. **The Sudoku puzzle that you have been working on for what seems like an eternity appears to be going swimmingly until you put the last number in place and see to your horror that there are two fives in the same square. Do you?**

   a) Sigh 'Oh dear' and start another puzzle.

   b) Glare at the answers in the back of the book for several minutes in disbelief.

   c) Tear the puzzle book into a thousand pieces in a little temper tantrum.

   d) Dictate a letter of complaint to the publisher for obviously having made a printing error.

2. **Which of these do you most readily associate with a visit to your nearest park?**

   a) Families laughing and playing.

   b) Birds singing.

   c) Seats covered in pigeon poop.

3. **While playing a board game with friends, do you struggle to hide your rising resentment when one of your opponents keeps throwing a six on the dice?**

4. **Would you take up astronomy?**
   a) To study the stars.
   b) To spy on your neighbours.

5. **You are invited to a party by friends. At what time do you start looking at your watch, ready to go home for a good night's sleep?**
   a) 8.30 pm.
   b) 10 pm.
   c) 1 am.

6. **A friend suggests you visit an art gallery together. Do you say?**
   a) 'Yes, I love looking around galleries.'
   b) 'I've never visited one before, but it will be good to broaden my mind and take in some culture for a change.'
   c) 'Okay, so long as the paintings are not full of cherubs. I can't stand cherubs.'
   d) 'Is it free to get in?'

7. **Would you only agree to go to an art gallery if they allowed you to improve some of the paintings, 'because that Edvard Munch just doesn't know how to draw a human face. It looks more like a bloody light bulb to me! And don't get me started on Picasso. Has he ever seen a real cat?'**

8. **From personal experience, which of these makes the best projectile?**

   a) A frisbee.

   b) A paper airplane.

   c) A computer keyboard.

9. **Do you refuse to go on fairground bumper cars because you feel that they encourage reckless driving and do not place sufficient emphasis on the virtues of signalling and using one's rear-view mirror?**

10. **In what room are you most likely to be found at a friend's house party?**

    a) The lounge, at the heart of all the dancing.

    b) The kitchen, so that you can enjoy a constant supply of food.

    c) Wherever the coats are, so that you can be ready to make a quick getaway.

11. **Do you consider a bracing walk over rolling hills to be . . .?**

    a) Healthy and invigorating.

    b) A quick way of catching a cold.

12. **Whereas many of your friends collect stamps or coins, have you become so lazy that the only thing you now collect is dust?**

13. Do you think bird watching is . . .?

    a) An enjoyable way of getting out and about with nature.

    b) A lot of time spent shivering in the cold while peering through binoculars at specks in the distance that fly off just as you are about to focus on them.

    c) Only any fun if you're a cat.

14. Have you reached the stage in life where a 'night on the tiles' refers to an evening game of Scrabble?

15. On a day out at a theme park, your family want you to ride with them on a scary roller coaster. Do you say?

    a) 'Sure, I'm all for it. I love the kick from a big adrenaline rush.'

    b) 'No, thanks. I don't want to ride on anything that goes faster than a donkey.'

    c) 'No, thanks. If I want to scare myself half to death, I can just read my latest energy bill.'

THE HOME

1. **If you find a cobweb near the ceiling of a room that your partner has just cleaned, how likely are you to mention it to her?**
    a) Extremely unlikely – it's easy to miss the odd cobweb, and in any case she'd just say: 'If you think you can do better, you know where the dust cloth is!'
    b) Perhaps, but only in passing – not as an accusation of general housekeeping incompetence.
    c) Almost certainly – it's points in the bank for the next time she accuses me of not putting dirty socks in the wash basket, leaving the lid off the cookie jar or forgetting to put the toilet seat down.

2. **While attempting to hang wallpaper, have you ever . . .?**
    a) Vowed that you'll never try to hang wallpaper again.
    b) Felt like one half of Laurel and Hardy.
    c) Screamed in frustration on discovering that what you thought was a bubble in the wallpaper was actually the cat.
    d) Deliberately torn the wallpaper in the hope that your partner would suggest painting the room instead.
    e) Thrown the pasting brush across the room in anger.
    f) Blamed a small child for getting the measurements wrong.
    g) Been threatened with divorce.

3. **If, following a particularly stressful wallpaper-hanging experience, your partner suggests that next time you should pay for professionals to come and do the decorating, do you reply?**
   a) 'Yes, that's a good idea.'
   b) 'I'll think about it.' – which actually means 'No, but I don't want to argue about it with you right now.'
   c) 'I'm not *paying* for someone to do it. I'm perfectly capable of doing it myself, you know.'

4. **After you have finished painting the ceiling and walls of the hallway, you ask your partner to tell you whether you may have missed anything. Do you become visibly annoyed if she takes your words at face value and finds more than half a dozen faults in your handiwork?**

5. **Have you ever accused any of your children of treating the family home like a hotel?**

6. **A neighbour's car alarm goes off in the middle of the night for the third time in a week. Do you?**
   a) Get out of bed and check that everything is okay.
   b) Pull the covers over your head to try and shut out the noise.
   c) Pray that somebody does actually steal it so the ruddy alarm won't keep going off in the middle of the night.

7. **After painstakingly putting together an item of self-assembly furniture over a period of three days and four mental breakdowns, you find that there are two parts left over. Do you?**

   a) Say nothing, hide them in a drawer and pray that the whole thing doesn't suddenly collapse.

   b) Try to ignore the error until the perfectionist in you gnaws away at your conscience and demands that, amid much huffing, puffing and tutting, you take it apart and start all over again.

8. **After your partner has finished cleaning and dusting the lounge, you notice that one of the pictures on the wall is very slightly crooked. Do you?**

   a) Ignore it.

   b) Straighten it without saying anything.

   c) Straighten it but make a point of letting her know that you had to straighten it because she had left it crooked.

9. **If a neighbour asks to borrow your power drill for the day, would you say?**

   a) 'Yes, of course.'

   b) 'No, buy your own.'

   c) 'Yes' on condition that he signs a formal contract covering the loan, including a clause stipulating that you will be paid a fee for every hour exceeding the mutually agreed twenty-four-hour limit for the return of the goods.

10. **Have you ever been involved in a full-on, no-holds-barred, wrestling match with three or more wire coat hangers that have become tangled up in the wardrobe?**

11. **You have just finished the laborious task of replacing the external sealant around your windows when your neighbour informs you that the product you have used is not very durable and that he knows a much better one. Do you?**
a) Thank him for the helpful suggestion.
b) Say that you'll bear that in mind (without really meaning it).
c) Spend the rest of the day planning your revenge on him for being such a smartarse.

12. **A stranger's car is parked on the street outside your house for most of the day. Do you?**
a) Ignore it, because it's a public highway and anyone is allowed to park there.
b) Consider it an infringement of your privacy, even though you realize you have no legal grounds for complaint.
c) Fuss about it all day, going to the window every five minutes to see if the car has finally moved. Arrange your armchair in a position that affords a clear view of the vehicle so that you can identify the owner in the event of a repeat offence.
d) Pin a note on the car windshield, reading 'PLEASE DO NOT PARK HERE AGAIN'.

13. **Has your partner ever asked you to put the cover on the double duvet and then found you fifteen minutes later thrashing about angrily inside the cover, desperately trying to escape?**

14. **Your neighbours host a boisterous party that's still in full swing at one o'clock in the morning. Is your chief motivation for calling the police to complain?**
    a) Because the level of noise is inconsiderate at that time of night.
    b) Because you were the only neighbours who weren't invited.

15. **When a friend calls at your home, what is the first thing you are likely to say?**
    a) 'Hello. Come in. It's good to see you.'
    b) 'Hello. Come in. Wipe your feet.'

16. **When you visit a friend's house for the first time, do you instinctively seek out signs of bad workmanship so that you can feel better about your own feeble attempts at DIY?**

17. **You have been looking forward to a nice, long, warm bath all day, but when you run it there is barely enough hot water to cover your ankles. When you emerge surprisingly quickly and your partner asks whether everything was okay, do you?**
    a) Say: 'I should have turned the hot water on sooner.'
    b) Mumble 'It was fine' in a tone that demands she probe further to unearth the root of your dissatisfaction.
    c) Leave her in no doubt as to the hardship and suffering you have just endured, interspersed with the occasional forced shiver of a magnitude not experienced since Captain Scott's last days in the Antarctic.

18. **You can't find your car keys, and after five minutes of increasingly bad-tempered searching, you ask your partner what she has done with them. She immediately locates them on the shelf where they always are, but partly obscured by a junk mail letter. Do you?**
    a) Thank her sincerely, admitting that you should have conducted a more thorough search of the area.
    b) Thank her grudgingly, while remaining unconvinced that you were negligent in any way.
    c) Accuse her of deliberately moving the keys to a spot where she knew you wouldn't be able to find them.

19. **Have you ever asked yourself why the toughest, most durable component of the new frying pan you have bought is the price sticker that you want to remove from the base? It never peels away in its entirety, but instead leaves behind unsightly sticky remnants, which, no matter how hard you wash, scrub or poke them, cling on like limpets for the next few months.**

20. **When do you consider it acceptable for the central heating to be switched on in your home?**
    a) As soon as anybody else complains that they are feeling a bit cold.
    b) When the house is so cold that the cat seeks refuge in the fridge because it is warmer in there.
    c) When someone's teeth start chattering – even though at the time they're in a glass on the bedside table.
    d) When somebody's face starts to turn blue and ice forms on their top lip.
    e) As soon as you feel cold.

21. **Have you ever inwardly screamed after sitting down on the toilet and then finding that the roll of paper has run out mid-wipe?**

22. **At the time, did it seem like the worst moment in your entire life when you stepped out of the shower, only to realize that you had forgotten to place a towel within easy reach? You then had to pad around the house, getting colder by the second and dripping water in**

your wake, in search of the nearest dry towel, a tough
mission which you feel would have tested the likes of
Bear Grylls or Chuck Norris.

23. **Which of these makes a constant whining noise in
your home?**
a) Air conditioning system.
b) Tumble dryer.
c) You.

LAW AND ORDER

1. **Which of the following do you consider to be an appropriate punishment for putting a non-recyclable item into the recycling bin?**

   a) A mild reprimand.

   b) A fine.

   c) Hanging, drawing and quartering.

2. **Which of these expressions have you used over the past twelve months?**

   a) 'A damn good thrashing never did me any harm!'

   b) 'A spell in the military is what they need!'

   c) 'They should bring back the cat o' nine tails!'

3. When doing jury service, do you think that it is your moral duty to find the defendant guilty regardless of the evidence because otherwise bringing the case to court is a waste of taxpayers' money?

4. Which of these fictional detectives do you think most accurately reflects the ability of the average twenty-first century police officer?
   a) Theo Kojak.
   b) Lieutenant Columbo.
   c) Inspector Clouseau.

5. Do you report so many inconsequential things to the police that you have the number of the local police station on speed dial and there is an interview room there named after you?

6. Do you immediately suspect that anyone seen standing outside your house for more than two minutes is . . .?
   a) Innocently waiting for someone.
   b) Looking for somewhere to have an emergency pee.
   c) Casing the joint.

7. Do you think it's a shame that the rack, the foot screw and bodily impalement have all fallen out of favour as acceptable methods of punishment?

8. Have you ever considered taking legal action over any of the following?

a) A bad haircut.

b) A grandchild stepping on your foot.

c) Someone you felt was encroaching on your personal space.

d) A game of Monopoly.

e) An unexpectedly powerful tap in a public toilet that soaks the front of your trousers to leave the impression that you didn't quite make it there in time.

f) Jehovah's Witnesses turning up on your doorstep uninvited.

g) A family member secretly eating the last chocolate in the box – the one which you had set your heart on.

h) Someone stopping unexpectedly at the top or bottom of an escalator.

i) An email falsely claiming that attractive Russian women living in your area were desperate to meet you.

j) Anyone taking a selfie.

k) Anyone guilty of poor umbrella etiquette.

l) An ominous horoscope.

m) Catching a cold from a member of your family.

n) Finding that someone else's spent firework has landed in your garden.

o) Someone deliberately rubbing their fingers on a balloon to make an annoying noise.

p) Someone who pushes in ahead of you while you are waiting to be served at the bar.

q) Someone failing to take their backpack into account when turning around directly in front of you.

r) A friend forgetting to send you a birthday card.

s) Completing a three-thousand-piece jigsaw puzzle, only to find there is a piece missing.

t) An overcooked steak in a restaurant.

u) An overcooked steak at home.

MONEY

1. **Your daughter asks you for a sizeable loan until pay day. Do you?**
   a) Agree unconditionally.
   b) Agree, but only after running it past your financial adviser to check that it's a worthwhile investment.
   c) Agree, but charge her interest.

2. **Have you ever given your partner a weekly housekeeping allowance and fined her if she exceeded the limit?**

3. **Your bank wants you to operate your account online in future. Are you ...?**
   a) Happy to give it a try, especially as your local branch with humans has closed.
   b) Sceptical, but you feel you don't really have a choice.
   c) Extremely reluctant. You have only recently learned to embrace the wheel and electricity, so online banking is definitely an innovation too far.

4. **While using an ATM, you are aware that the person next in line is standing close enough behind you to see you enter your PIN. Do you?**

    a) Ignore them and carry out the transaction as swiftly as possible.

    b) Turn around and glare at them.

    c) Turn around and ask them if they would mind stepping back a little.

    d) Turn around and, like a referee at a soccer match, measure back three paces to where you think they ought to be standing.

5. **Have you ever told the person in front of you at the ATM to hurry up because their transaction seems to have lasted at least five minutes? What are they keying in? The script to *Gone with the Wind*? And then, when their money finally comes through, they have to study it as if they've never seen bank notes before! Get on with it! Some of us have got lives to lead.**

6. **You come downstairs one morning to find that none of the lights in your kitchen are working, leaving you with the prospect of having to call out an expensive electrician. Do you?**

    a) Call an electrician anyway, deciding that it is a necessary, if unwelcome, expense.

    b) Keep switching the lights on and off in the hope that the problem will somehow fix itself. After all, it's what they recommend for computers.

  c) Attempt the repairs yourself, make a complete mess
of it, lose your temper, and end up incurring more
expense than if you had called out an electrician in the
first place.

**7. Do you angrily tear up the letter when the same bank
that charges you an exorbitant fee for every day you
are overdrawn by even the smallest amount, keeps
sending you offers for loans and exclusive platinum
credit cards?**

**8. While shopping in town you need the toilet, but find
that there is a charge to use it. Do you?**

  a) Pay up without complaint.

  b) Pay up with a grumble.

  c) Stubbornly hold it in until you can go behind a
discreetly located bush.

9. **Have you ever thought that you seem to be the only person in the world who still carries cash, because you are fed up with having to wait an eternity at the bar while the person in front of you pays for his bottle of overpriced sparkling water by credit card?**

10. **When you see a charity fundraiser lurking in the street waiting to pounce, do you?**
    a) Stop and listen to their pitch and, if you feel the cause is worthy, make a financial contribution.
    b) Rush past them without making eye contact, saying, whether it is true or not: 'Sorry, I'm in a hurry.'
    c) Wait until they have collared an unsuspecting passer-by and then swerve around them on their blind side so they do not even notice you. Result!

11. **Have you ever seriously considered hibernation as a means of keeping down the cost of your winter fuel?**

12. **Have you ever wanted to tell your children that the Bank of Mum and Dad has closed down and been replaced by a fast food takeaway?**

MOVIES

1. **When you saw that Bambi's mother had been killed, did you think?**
   a) 'How sad.'
   b) 'Venison for dinner.'

2. **How regularly do you go to the cinema to see a new film?**
   a) Fairly often. I like to keep up with modern pop culture.
   b) Only in winter if I want to find somewhere warm for the afternoon.
   c) I prefer to wait a couple of years until it is shown on TV, when I can watch it for free and without the guy in the row behind talking all the way through, spraying the back of my neck with popcorn.
   d) I stopped going to the movies when they introduced women into westerns.

3. **Watching the famous shower scene in *Psycho*, did you think?**
   a) 'That was brilliant.'
   b) 'That was unnecessarily violent.'
   c) 'That was an appalling waste of water.'

4. Did you always feel that Grumpy received an unfairly bad press in *Snow White and the Seven Dwarfs* because he actually adopted a far more realistic approach to life than Happy – and you do children no favours by encouraging unsubstantiated optimism concerning the many challenges that lay ahead of them?

5. **During *The Sound of Music*, were you hoping that the Von Trapp family would be captured before they had the chance to burst into song again?**

6. **Do you think moviegoers who applaud at the end of a film are . . .?**
   a) Admirable, because they are showing their appreciation for all the hard work that has gone into making the movie.
   b) Stupid, because neither the actors nor the director can hear them.

7. **With which Muppet characters do you most closely identify?**
   a) Kermit.
   b) Fozzie Bear.
   c) Statler and Waldorf.

8. **When the monster burst through John Hurt's stomach in *Alien*, did you think that the greatest tragedy was that it had ruined a perfectly good white T-shirt?**

9. **Did you feel that Cinderella had ideas above her station and that any decent girl of her age should have been safely tucked up in bed long before midnight anyway?**

MUSIC

1. **Your grandson says he really likes modern rap music. Would you?**
   a) Encourage him.
   b) Tolerate him.
   c) Disinherit him.

2. **Does your music collection contain anything from the twenty-first century?**

3. **Do you think hip-hop is?**
   a) A type of music.
   b) Something your neighbour had done in hospital last year.

4. **Have you ever grumbled when TV ads for Father's Day recommend buying presents such as Perry Como CDs, when in that period of history you were into the Rolling Stones?**

5. **Have you used any of these terms recently?**
   a) Hit parade.
   b) Beat combo.
   c) Disc jockey.

d) Swinging.

e) Groovy.

f) Fab.

g) Gramophone record.

h) With it.

6. **Have you ever sung the praises of opera but then criticized pop music because 'you can't understand any of the words'?**

7. **A friend has acquired a karaoke machine and asks you to perform a duet. Do you say?**
   a) 'Why not? I've always fancied myself as a latter-day Sinatra.'
   b) 'Well, I don't mind making a fool of myself if you don't.'
   c) 'Sorry, I can feel a sore throat coming on.'
   d) 'To be perfectly honest, I'd rather stick pins in my eyes than sing karaoke.'

8. **Do you think Taylor Swift is someone who makes suits while you wait?**

9. **Which of these do you hate?**
   a) Singers on TV who are clearly miming.
   b) Singers on TV who are brave enough to perform live, but you object because the sound is not as perfect as on the CD.
   c) All singers.

10. Do you agree with the definition of a gentleman as being 'someone who knows how to play the bagpipes, but doesn't'?

11. Which, if any, of the following have you heard of?
    a) Drake.
    b) Stormzy.
    c) Tinie Tempah.
    d) Jason Derulo.
    e) Nicki Minaj.
    f) Iggy Azalea.
    g) Blink-182.
    h) Lil Kim
    i) 50 Cent.
    j) Foo Fighters.
    k) The Monkees.

Then   Now

12. Have you ever had a hissy fit over a pair of earphones that have somehow become tangled? They were fine when you put them away neatly in the drawer two days earlier, but now the leads are wrapped around each other like a nest of copulating vipers. By the time you finally manage to untangle them, your window for listening to music has inevitably passed.

13. When confronted with the younger generation's music, have you ever said: 'Who put this rubbish on? Let's have something decent.'

14. In your opinion, what is the best thing about a cello?

a) No other musical instrument can invoke such a sense of melancholy and raw emotion.

b) It burns easily.

15. Do you feel that the phasing out of vinyl records marked the beginning of the end of civilization as we know it?

16. Which of these things do you miss most about vinyl records?

a) Their texture, shape and feel.

b) The unadulterated pleasure of placing one carefully on the turntable and lowering the stylus.

c) Their tendency to warp if left in a sunny spot, especially on the back seat of a car.

d) The irreparable scratch that would inevitably ruin your favourite album track.

17. Do you feel that 'dad dancing' is a much under-rated art form?

POLITICS

1. **How would you best describe Donald Trump's face?**

   a) Statesmanlike.

   b) Orange.

   c) Punchable.

2. **It is election time, and the local candidate calls at your house asking for your support. Do you?**

   a) Listen attentively to the points he is making, regardless of whether you agree with them.

   b) Tell him that you're busy and shut the door in his face.

   c) Set the dogs on him.

3. **How can you tell when a politician is lying?**
   a) His face turns red.
   b) He develops a facial tick.
   c) His lips move.

4. **When a political leader states that the allegations about a member of his administration are totally, utterly and completely untrue, does he mean?**
   a) 'I firmly believe the allegations are untrue.'
   b) 'I really hope the allegations are untrue.'
   c) 'The allegations are true, but nobody's ever going to be able to prove a thing.'

5. **Your daughter's latest boyfriend has opposing political views to yours. When he comes to visit, do you?**
   a) Steer the conversation away from politics for the sake of peace and harmony.
   b) Grumble endlessly about his political beliefs.
   c) Tell him he's barred from the house until he signs a full recantation.

6. **When during a live TV debate a politician says, 'With all due respect to my colleague', does he mean?**
   a) 'In general, I do respect his views, but in this instance I fundamentally disagree with him.'
   b) 'I have no respect whatsoever for my colleague, but I am trying to appear polite and civilized in a desperate attempt to win public sympathy.'
   c) 'Don't listen to that idiot, listen to this idiot.'

7. **When you see a politician kiss a baby at election time, do you think?**
   a) 'He's showing his gentle, paternal side.'
   b) 'He'll do absolutely anything to win a vote.'
   c) 'He's just one step away from eating it.'

8. **If you were flying in a hot air balloon with Donald Trump, Bill Clinton and Tony Blair at an altitude of five thousand feet and urgently needed to jettison something over the side to prevent the balloon crashing to the ground, which of the occupants would you choose to save?**
   a) Donald Trump.
   b) Bill Clinton.
   c) Tony Blair.
   d) The sandbag.

9. **If, following a scandal, a politician calls for a thorough, independent review, does he mean?**
   a) 'We are going to conduct a thorough, independent review.'
   b) 'We are going to conduct a thorough, independent review but we may not make the results public if we don't like them.'
   c) 'We are busy rushing around to cover up any incriminating evidence.'

10. Do you always vote at elections?

 a) Yes, because I want my views to be represented by the best available candidate.

 b) No, because all politicians are equally useless.

 c) Yes, because if I don't bother to vote, I won't have the right to complain later about what a useless idiot the winner turned out to be.

11. Which of these do you think would be the ideal position for Nigel Farage?

 a) UK Prime Minister.

 b) UK Foreign Secretary.

 c) Hanging from a lamp-post.

RELATIONSHIPS

1. You have a minor disagreement with your partner in which you are unequivocally at fault. How long does it take you to admit that you might just conceivably be in the wrong . . . on this occasion?
   a) Fifteen minutes.
   b) One hour.
   c) Six months.

2. Would you find your partner's habit of gently sighing in her sleep . . .?
   a) Relaxing.
   b) Endearing.
   c) Irritating.

3. Do you consider your own habit of snoring loudly like a rampant stag during the rutting season to be . . .?
   a) Annoying.
   b) Unavoidable.
   c) Entertaining.

4. Your partner lazily turns over in bed in the middle of a winter's night and, in doing so, pulls the duvet off you. Do you?

a) Suffer in silence and freeze.

b) Gently try and ease part of the duvet back over to your side without waking her.

c) Yank the duvet back – with interest.

d) Elbow her firmly in the ribs to wake her and tell her what she has done.

5. **You say something to your partner in another room, but she can't hear you properly and calls back: 'What did you say?' How many times are you willing to repeat it before you finally give up and yell in frustration: 'It doesn't matter. Forget it'?**

a) Twice.

b) Three times.

c) Four times or more until she eventually hears you and calls back: 'There's no need to shout.'

6. **Your partner tells you off for always putting the can opener in the wrong drawer after use. Do you?**

a) Apologize, and promise that you'll try to remember in future.

b) Tell her: 'I thought it looked happier in there.'

c) Tell her: 'You should count yourself lucky I put anything away.'

d) Silently seethe, while composing a list of things she does that irritate you, ready to be unleashed at the next confrontation.

7. **You see a couple kissing and cuddling in public. Do you think?**

a) 'How nice to see two people in love.'

b) 'They should be more discreet and get a room.'

c) 'I don't see the point in extravagant displays of affection. What's wrong with a good old-fashioned handshake?'

8. **Your partner suddenly suggests making love on the lounge carpet just as you were about to watch the golf on the TV. Do you?**

a) Switch off the TV so that you can concentrate solely on the matter in hand.

b) Say that sex with your partner is far more important than the TV, but record the golf anyway.

c) Carefully position yourself during lovemaking so that you have an unobstructed view of the TV screen, while taking care to play the right hole and not stray out of bounds.

9. **It's a popular misconception that only women invent headaches as a reason for not having sex. Have you ever used any of these as an excuse for not wanting to make love with your partner?**

a) 'My horoscope for today does not indicate that physical contact should be high on my agenda.'

b) 'A neighbour might call round wanting to borrow something.'

c) 'I was going to wash the car.'

d) 'I was going to delouse the cat.'

e) 'The phone might ring.'

f) 'The voices in my head are telling me "no".'

g) 'It's a bit cold for all that.'

h) 'It will be too hot and sweaty – and I've only just washed my hair.'

i) 'I don't want to crumple the newly ironed bed sheets.'

j) 'You look tired.'

k) 'The noise from the builders across the road will put me off.'

l) 'I'm never very good on a Thursday.'

m) 'All the neighbours will know what we're up to if I draw the bedroom curtains in the middle of the day.'

n) 'I might get cramp.'

o) 'The dog might try and join in again.'

p) 'I don't know about you, but it just doesn't seem right – not in church, especially with all the mourners watching.'

10. **Your partner makes it known that she wants you to give her a big surprise for her birthday. Do you?**
    a) Plan a secret party.
    b) Plan a secret trip abroad – with her.
    c) Plan a secret trip abroad – without her.
    d) Plan a threesome.
    e) Deliberately forget her birthday for the first time ever and wait to see if that constitutes a big enough surprise.

11. **As the father of the bride who, even in these times of equality, is still expected to pay for all things related to the 'big day', do you despair that so many weddings suddenly seem unable to proceed without the expensive services of a wedding planner? 'We'll take away all the stress of arranging the wedding,' they claim, while simultaneously adding extra stress in the form of a sizeable hole in your bank account.**

12. **In general, would your level of interest in the news that a so-called celebrity couple are splitting up be . . .?**
    a) Considerable.
    b) Average.
    c) Marginally less than their interest would be in the colour, shape and constitution of your last bowel movement.

13. Have you ever bought any of the following as a present for your partner?

a) A pair of oven gloves.

b) A set of bathroom scales.

c) A potato peeler.

d) A verruca treatment kit.

e) A family sized bottle of toilet cleaner.

f) A set of screwdrivers.

g) A vacuum cleaner.

h) A jar of anti-wrinkle cream.

i) A framed picture of yourself ... with an old girlfriend.

j) An air freshener.

k) A set of wooden spoons.

l) Tampons.

m) Gym membership ... when she hasn't asked for it.

n) A pack of dust cloths.

o) A season ticket for *your* favourite football team.

p) Any other gift that immediately started an argument.

SERVICES

1. **The newspaper boy delivers the wrong newspaper to your house. Do you?**
   a) Accept it anyway.
   b) Walk round to the shop and politely point out the mistake.
   c) March round to the shop and leave the owner in no doubt as to the boy's incompetence.
   d) Chase the paper boy down the street, shouting and cursing and strongly implying that his mother was a female dog.

2. **Your window cleaner leaves a small smear on the window pane. Do you?**
   a) Wipe it off.
   b) Ignore it.
   c) Fret about it all day until your partner gets so fed up with you droning on about it that *she* wipes it off.

3. **An eagerly awaited parcel fails to arrive at your home on the promised day and, after spending two-and-a-half hours on the phone to the delivery company, you learn that it has been sent to a completely different address two hundred miles away. Do you tell the company . . .?**

a) 'Don't worry, I'll drive there to fetch it. It will be a nice day out for us.'

b) 'I suppose I should be grateful that you actually bothered to deliver it to something resembling a house and didn't just dump it at the side of the road.'

c) 'It's a good job your company wasn't around at the time of the Nativity – or the Three Wise Men would have had to tell Mary and Joseph: "We've got the gold and the frankincense, but the myrrh won't be arriving until Tuesday!"'

4. **When you take your car in to be repaired, are you of the general opinion that the garage mechanic makes up your bill as he goes along?**

5. **Have you ever paid for your annual car service without querying at least two-thirds of the cost?**

6. **If you take your car to a garage for four new tyres and the mechanic tells you to come back and collect it the next day, have you ever complained: 'How come it takes you twenty-four hours? They do it in under thirty seconds at the race track!'**

7. **Would you take offence if a garage mechanic looked at your ample waist and said: 'I don't need to ask where you keep your spare tyre'?**

8. **When workmen are at your house, do you?**
   a) Offer to make them a hot drink.
   b) Make them go without because if they were so desperate for a drink they should have brought their own flask. Besides, you want them to get on with the job, not keep stopping for drink breaks.

9. **If a workman walks on your lounge carpet without first removing his shoes, do you instinctively retrace his footsteps when he has gone to check that he hasn't marked it in any way?**

10. **You get up early because a workman is supposed to arrive at your house at 8.30 am. He has still not arrived by 9 am. How regularly after that do you check your watch?**
    a) Every twenty minutes.
    b) Every ten minutes.
    c) Every thirty seconds.

11. **Does your heart sink when you realize that, in order for your customer complaint to be registered, you must call a foreign call centre and thus conduct a two-way conversation where neither party is able to understand the other?**

12. **Is your default position on tradespeople in general that they are?**

    a) All trying to earn an honest day's pay for an honest day's work.

    b) All trying to rip you off.

13. **Have you ever sighed, 'I must be in the wrong job,' after contacting plumbers and electricians to carry out emergency repairs, only to hear that they're all too busy for the next two months?**

14. Which of these never fail to give you the hump?

a) Workmen at your home who disappear for two hours at lunchtime.

b) Workmen at your home who finish for the day partway through the afternoon, when there are still two more hours of daylight left.

c) Workmen who climb on to your roof to replace a loose tile and find five other jobs that need doing while they are up there, safe in the knowledge that you are unable to contradict them from your ground-level viewpoint.

d) Uninvited salespeople who call at your home to try and sell you new windows when the ones you already have are less than three months old.

e) Workmen who ask if they can park their van on your newly laid driveway – but the van then proceeds to leak drops of oil all over it.

f) Workmen who are unable to identify the purpose of the perfectly placed doorbell six inches to their right and instead hammer on your door in a manner liable to raise the dead.

g) Workmen at your home who don't clean up afterwards.

h) Workmen who make a half-hearted attempt to clean up but still leave your home looking like a bomb site.

i) Workmen who sing or whistle out of tune.

j) Workmen at your home who ask for a speciality tea or coffee, whether you're making one or not. In the old days, they just used to request a mug of strong coffee with twelve sugars. Since when did they get so picky? Where do they think they are – Starbucks? They'll be wanting you to bring out the best china next.

k) Workmen who, in bending down, cause their jeans to drop so low and expose so much buttock flesh that an unsuspecting passer-by might be tempted to park her bicycle there.

l) Workmen who call you 'mate' or 'buddy' when you are neither to them.

m) Workmen who ask if they can use your toilet and then proceed to dump three days' worth of human waste down your bowl, leaving behind not only a stench that would have the average skunk reaching for the air freshener but also more skid marks than you see at the Indy 500.

SHOPPING

1. **At the supermarket's automated checkout, you can't complete the procedure because the machine is unable to distinguish an apple from an avocado. Do you?**

   a) Patiently try again.

   b) Call an assistant to help.

   c) Violently kick the machine while screaming: 'Don't you know the difference between a bloody apple and an avocado? I thought you were supposed to be intelligent! Did an avocado ever fall on Isaac Newton's head to inspire his theory of gravity? Does an avocado a day keep the doctor away? And when was the last time you went bobbing for avocados?!'

2. **How often do you consider that a trip into town has only been worth the effort if you have returned home with at least three things to gripe about?**
   a) Every time.
   b) Occasionally.
   c) Never.

3. **When buying electrical goods, are you more likely to?**
   a) Succumb to the sales clerk's pressure pitch by paying extra to purchase a warranty for peace of mind.
   b) Firmly decline the offer of a warranty as a waste of money, giving the sales clerk a piece of your mind.

4. **When standing in line at the express checkout in the supermarket, how often do you count the number of items in other shoppers' baskets to ensure that they have obeyed the rule of eight items or fewer.**
   a) Always.
   b) Occasionally.
   c) Never.

5. **When you see a line of bargain stores, charity shops and nail bars, do you think to yourself: 'I can remember when this street had proper shops'?**

6. **When you walk into a store and a sales assistant immediately pounces on you with the dreaded words 'Can I help you?', would you be more likely to say?**
    a) 'I'm just looking, thanks.'
    b) 'How kind of you! I'm looking for a device that will make me invisible to sales assistants. Do you have any?'
    c) 'No. Go away and leave me to shoplift in peace.'

7. **Have you ever entered a clothing store, only to be forced out again within seconds because you found the music unbearably loud and not to your taste?**

8. **As you leave a store, the sales assistant who has just served you gushes, with enough syrup to drown a flapjack: 'Have a nice day!' Do you reply?**
    a) 'And you.'
    b) 'I'll try, but you're immediately putting pressure on me.'
    c) 'I would if people like you didn't keep telling me to have a nice day.'

9. **If a shop assistant gives you the wrong change, do you instinctively think?**
    a) 'I'm sure it was an innocent mistake.'
    b) 'He was trying to swindle me!'

10. **Have you ever sought out the store detective to report that someone has abandoned their shopping cart randomly in the supermarket parking lot instead of returning it to its allotted zone?**

11. **You are pushing a shopping cart around the supermarket, but the shopper directly in front of you is really slow. When she stops suddenly – for the third time – do you?**
    a) Just accept that it will take a little longer to complete your shopping this week.
    b) Sigh loudly in the hope that she realizes she has irritated you.
    c) Swerve around her and then cut her up the other side.
    d) Ram her heels with your cart to show her who is lord of the aisles.

12. **Have you ever walked into a shop, forgotten what it was that you wanted to buy, grumbled at the sales assistant because she didn't know either, and then walked out again in a huff?**

13. **While waiting in line at the supermarket checkout, which of the following make you see red?**
    a) Seeing that another line is moving much faster than yours, prompting you to tell your partner repeatedly, 'I said we should have got in that line,' even though you had only thought it rather than actually mentioned it out loud.
    b) Seeing that the customer in front of you has done what appears to be their annual shop on a quiet weekday morning, loading their cart with enough cans of food to stock a nuclear fallout bunker for the next five years.
    c) Waiting patiently for twenty minutes and then seeing

the cashier put up the 'till closed' sign just as you were about to place your items on the belt.

d) The customer in front of you deciding that they have picked up the wrong item and then returning to the shelves to find a replacement, thereby causing a five-minute delay.

e) Customers who don't have the loading/bagging/paying routine perfected with military precision and instead end up scrabbling in bags for their purse while their overripe pineapple leaks on to the bagging area, creating a sticky trap for everyone else's shopping.

14. **Do you scoff when you hear self-important people value their personal shopper more highly than their doctor?**

15. **When you buy a pair of shoes, do you become impatient when the sales assistant also tries to sell you?**
    a) Shoe cream.
    b) Water repellent shoe spray.
    c) A shoe cloth.
    d) A shoe tree.
    e) A shoe horn.
    f) Her old dishwasher.

SPORTS

1. **You endure a torrid afternoon on the golf course,
    losing five balls, a five-iron and two friends. Do you?**
    a) Blame yourself for making so many poor shots.
    b) Blame your clubs for making so many poor shots.
    c) Blame your partner for not forcing you to stay at home
       and decorate the bedroom.

2. **You lose both games of ping pong to your ten-year-old
    nephew. Do you?**
    a) Congratulate him on being such a good player.
    b) Say: 'How about we make it best of five?'
    c) Insist that you continue playing until you finally win
       a game, even if it means keeping the boy up until four
       o'clock in the morning.
    d) Slam your bat down on the table in anger, mutter
       something about cheating and storm off to the pub.

3. **Have you ever barracked sports competitors on TV
    so forcefully that your partner has threatened to
    confiscate the remote?**

4. **On whose behaviour do you model yourself on the tennis court?**
   a) Roger Federer.
   b) Bjorn Borg.
   c) John McEnroe.

5. **Do you think that only a tennis racket with a wooden frame is a proper racket?**

6. **Do you measure your expertise at golf by . . .?**
   a) How far you can hit the ball.
   b) How far you can throw the club after a bad shot.

7. **Has a jockey ever had to take out a restraining order on you after the horse he was riding (and on which you had bet) was beaten by a short head?**

8. **If motor racing is on TV, do you think?**
   a) 'Great. I love the thrills and spills of car racing.'

b) 'I can't be bothered. It's just lots of cars going round and round for two hours. It's not much different from a busy Saturday at a multi-storey car park.'

c) 'Let's see if there's something more exciting on the other channel, such as pro-celebrity knitting or a documentary on dog worming.'

9. **At least twice a week do you find yourself agreeing with Mark Twain's definition of golf as 'a good walk spoiled'?**

10. **Have you ever been tempted to go skiing?**
    a) Yes, it's an exhilarating experience.
    b) I might go for the après-ski if I can just sit around and watch all the other stuff.
    c) Why would I want to spend an arm and a leg just to break an arm and a leg?
    d) It's too much like knocking down trees with your face. Besides, I have no desire to participate in any sport where there are ambulances at the finish.

11. **While watching your favourite football team, have you ever audibly questioned the referee's . . .?**
    a) Eyesight.
    b) Neutrality.
    c) Parentage.

12. **Do you only enjoy watching ice skating if someone falls over?**

13. **In the clubhouse, are you best known among your fellow golfers for . . .?**
    a) Always buying a round of drinks.
    b) Always playing with a smile on your face, even when your divots go further than your shots and you seem to have spent more time in a bunker than Hitler.
    c) Never conceding a putt.

14. **Do you feel that there should be a one-game ban for any sports competitor who uses the word 'banter' – and two games for using the abbreviation 'bants'?**

15. **Do you consider angling to be . . .?**
    a) A chance to be at one with nature, a day spent in the fresh air away from the stresses of modern life.
    b) A waste of a day sat on a muddy riverbank in pouring rain trying to catch something that you end up throwing back in the water anyway. What's the point of that? And anyway, it's hardly anything to boast about that you managed to outwit a fish – a creature that never even got out of the evolutionary starting gate!

16. **Do you think the rules of synchronized swimming should stipulate that if one person drowns, the rest of the team should drown, too?**

17. In your opinion, which of these are not proper sports?

   a) Rhythmic gymnastics.

   b) Dressage.

   c) Darts.

   d) Cheerleading.

   e) Women's football.

18. Do you regularly tell your elderly, arthritic neighbour – in a manner not necessarily intended as a compliment – that even she could do a better job than your favourite football team's current manager/ goalkeeper/strikers?

19. How many times in the last season have you vowed never to go and watch your favourite team again?

   a) None.

   b) Once or twice.

   c) Every week.

TECHNOLOGY

1. **Your computer has not been loading properly for several weeks. What is your preferred method for dealing with a computer problem?**

    a) Do nothing and hope that it somehow resolves itself (Note: this rarely works).

    b) Phone an IT engineer (Note: this rarely works either and is more expensive).

    c) Shout and swear at the computer, occasionally resorting to acts of physical violence such as hitting the screen with a pad of Post-It notes.

    d) Scream: 'That's it, we're finished!' and throw the hard drive out of the window (Note: this, too, rarely works but is eminently more satisfying).

2. **Which of these do you think your family would choose for you as an appropriate internet username?**

    a) special1

    b) wonderfuldad1

    c) grumpy1

3. **Have you ever been timed out of a website simply because you took too long to remember the answers to your two memorable questions?**

4. **Do any of these internet features have you tearing out what remains of your hair?**

a) Adverts for shoes that pop up on every site you visit just because you recently bought a pair online. How many pairs of shoes do they think you need? Do they think you're a human millipede?

b) Sites that freeze on the payment page so you're never sure whether the transaction has been completed or not.

c) The interminable adverts that precede any sports video. You just want to watch the goals, not some guy showing off his skills with an electric screwdriver for two minutes.

d) Buffering.

e) The extended commercial breaks during online TV shows. On real TV, they say there is time to make a drink during an ad break, well, online you can almost go out for a three-course meal without missing a second of the action.

f) Pop-up adverts that hide their close buttons.

g) Adverts that are placed suspiciously close to the scroll-down key so that before you realize it, instead of reading a news story about a two-headed goat in Mongolia, you find you are about to buy a new car.

h) Newspaper websites that make you complete a meaningless marketing survey before you are allowed to read the story.

i) Websites that presume to know which books might be of future interest to you. Sure, you once bought a copy of *The Wind in the Willows* on Amazon but that doesn't mean you're suddenly eager to read books about amphibians, vintage motor cars, diseases that affect badgers, and rodent extermination.

5. **Have you ever become so confused by the wording on a website that you can't work out whether you're supposed to tick or untick the box saying that you're happy for your details to be passed on to relevant third parties and end up just exiting the site in a temper – and then dreading a stream of cold callers over the next few weeks pestering you about everything from pet insurance to erectile dysfunction?**

6. **Have you ever come to the conclusion that your computer's built-in troubleshooting facility is about as likely to solve your lack of internet access as Bugs Bunny is to bring lasting peace to the Middle East?**

7. **In your view, which of these innovations have been a force for evil rather than good?**
   a) The telephone.
   b) The motor car.
   c) The internet.

d) Television.

e) Space travel.

f) The microwave oven.

g) The mini skirt.

h) The skateboard.

i) McDonald's.

j) The video game.

k) Muzak.

l) Bubble wrap.

8. **If you speak to an IT engineer about a problem with your computer, do you become flustered when he or she talks to you as if you have a masters degree in software technology whereas in reality the only computer function you have mastered is the on/off button?**

9. **Would you be unable to buy anything on the internet, pay your energy bills online, access your online bank account or even send an email if you ever forgot the name of your first pet?**

10. **Do you know what the term 'app' is short for?**

a) Apparatus.

b) Apparition.

c) Application.

d) Appetiser.

e) Appendectomy.

11. Have you ever cursed a hand-drying machine in a public washroom that blasts out warm air but then automatically switches off after only three seconds? That's not long enough to dry average-sized hands thoroughly. Does it cater solely for toddlers?

12. Do you frequently get the feeling that if you picked up an elderly snail, placed it in a sea of thick glue and tied a ball and chain around its shell, it still wouldn't be as slow as your broadband speed?

13. Do you also get the feeling that there are days when it would be easier to gain access to the Pope's private bedroom in the Vatican or to the vaults in Fort Knox than to gain access to the internet on your computer?

14. Have you referred to your computer as 'a piece of worthless old junk' (or expressed similar sentiments towards it) at least once in the past seven days?

15. Can you understand why a new printer ink cartridge costs almost as much as a printer itself and why, drop for drop, printer ink seems to be more expensive than liquid gold?

16. In your experience, which of these crises takes the longest to resolve?
    a) Catalonia's push for independence from the rest of Spain.

b) The Hundred Years War.

c) A paper jam in your printer.

17. **Do you ever think your computer's printer is out to get you?**

18. **Do you sense a conspiracy when, just as you are at your busiest, your computer suddenly announces that it is doing updates . . . beginning with number one of fifty-two? Helpfully it informs you: 'This may take some time.'**

19. **Do you remain so wary of modern technology that you still prefer to use a manual typewriter and carbon paper to a computer keyboard?**

20. **Which of the following questions have ever exercised your mind?**
    a) 'What the hell is Pinterest?'
    b) 'What the hell is Tinder?'
    c) 'What the hell is Buzznet?'
    d) 'What the hell is Tumblr?'
    e) 'What the hell is Spotify?'
    f) 'What the hell is Flickr?'
    g) 'What the hell is Snapchat?'
    h) 'What the hell is Grindr?'
    i) 'What the hell is the internet?'

TELEVISION

1. **Someone on TV says something with which you strongly disagree. Do you?**
    a) Change channels.
    b) Accept that everyone is entitled to their own opinion, even if they are wrong.
    c) Call the person every name under the sun.
    d) Throw your carpet slipper at the set.

2. **Can you see the point of the Kardashians?**
    a) Yes – they're quite entertaining.
    b) No – they're awful.
    c) Who are the Kardashians?

3. **You and your partner are watching a TV thriller when, fifteen minutes from the end, you remember that you have seen it before. Do you?**
    a) Remain silent for fear of spoiling the ending for your partner.
    b) Say that you have seen it before but, even though it is killing you to keep quiet, refuse to elaborate – unless your partner becomes so infuriated by your smug expression that she demands to know.
    c) Coldly announce who the murderer is and flee into the kitchen.

4. **Is your favourite TV show?**
   a) A comedy.
   b) *Real Life Serial Killers*.
   c) Watching the footage from the dozen CCTV cameras you have installed around your house so that you can see what's going on in your street at night.

5. **Did you always feel that, no matter how honourable and chivalrous his intentions, Popeye the sailor man should have saved some of his can of spinach for the dangerously anorexic Olive Oyl, who clearly needed a substantial meal more than he did?**

6. **When someone describes their experience on a reality TV show as having been an 'amazing journey', do you think the description is only justified if they have caught at least a helicopter, a ferry, a rickshaw, two buses, a train and a camel to get there?**

7. **Which of these do you think is the ideal vehicle for Piers Morgan?**
   a) A talk show.
   b) A panel show.
   c) One without brakes.

8. **Have you ever been puzzled why vacuous celebrities are called reality TV stars when only in the minds of themselves and their agents are they 'stars' and their grip on reality is tenuous at best?**

9. **At the start of your favourite TV soap, the announcer warns that the following programme 'contains scenes which some viewers may find upsetting.' Do you think?**
   a) 'Thanks for the warning. I'll cover my eyes.'
   b) 'I think I can take it. After all, I served on the front line at the winter sales.'
   c) 'Well, then, why are you showing this stuff at seven o'clock in the evening when young children are likely to be watching?'

10. **Do you often find yourself yelling 'Not another one!' at what seems like an interminable TV ad break?**

11. **Which of these make you want to reach for the remote, turn the damn thing off and pick up a good book instead?**
   a) Distracting reminders about the *next* programme that pop up on your screen at a crucial point during the one you are watching.
   b) End credits that fly around so fast and in such small wording that they are impossible to read.
   c) A show that is repeated twice more on the same channel within the next five days in case you were lucky enough to miss it the first time around.
   d) Trailers for the next episode of a drama series that reveal way too much of the plot.
   e) Talent shows where every mediocre contestant is told they'll be a star.
   f) Gritty dramas with too much sex.

g) Gritty dramas with not enough sex.

h) Game shows that are repeated so soon after their original transmission that, even with your memory, you can still remember the answers.

i) A 'brand new Saturday night entertainment' show whose format is almost identical to its twelve short-lived predecessors.

j) Ad breaks that are much louder than the actual show, so that you have to keep adjusting the volume on the remote.

k) A comedy panel show that is essentially a repeat but is broadcast in a longer version to include items that weren't funny enough to make the original edit.

l) Shows that recap the 'story so far' after each ad break. How bad do they think your memory is that you need reminders every fifteen minutes? It's just a way of padding out the feeble content to fill an hour.

m) Celebrities who burst into tears over nothing more serious than a broken fingernail as soon as a microphone is placed in front of them.

n) Any shopping channel.

12. **Do you find yourself frequently groaning: 'A hundred and fifteen channels and not one decent thing to watch!'?**

13. **Your partner enters the room while you are watching an eagerly anticipated TV sports show, and then proceeds to talk to you all the way through it. Do you?**
    a) Reply concisely but courteously without taking your eyes off the screen.
    b) Answer the first couple of questions but then ignore the next in the hope that she gets the message.
    c) Threaten to invite a Caribbean steel band round to play during the next episode of her favourite show.

14. **Has your enjoyment of Yogi Bear always been tempered by the concern that two dangerous, wild animals having such close interaction with humans could only lead to environmental and health problems for the wider community?**

15. **When you hear someone on TV misuse the word 'literally', does it make your blood boil – but not literally?**

16. **Your daughter comes to stay for a few days and takes control of the TV remote. Do you?**
    a) Happily allow it, so that she can choose whatever channel she wants to watch.
    b) Quietly smoulder with indignation.
    c) Regain custody of it the moment she steps out of the room and promise never to let it out of your grasp again.

TRAVEL

1. **Even though he is wearing headphones, the music on a young man's iPod is clearly audible in your train coach. Do you?**

   a) Politely ask him to turn the sound down a little.

   b) Join in and start dancing in the aisle.

   c) Glare at him contemptuously and report him to the train guard at the first possible opportunity.

2. **Your flight has been delayed for six hours, and the airline announcement apologizes for any inconvenience this may cause to passengers. Do you believe the airline . . .?**

   a) Is genuinely remorseful because it prides itself on customer satisfaction.

   b) Is remorseful only because it fears the bad publicity.

   c) Couldn't really give a toss.

3. **When approaching the ePassport reader machine at airport Arrivals, how confident are you that the much-vaunted, hi-tech facial recognition technology will work?**

   a) Extremely confident. Modern technology is wonderful.

   b) A little apprehensive, because last time your beard and

bald pate led the machine to inform you that your head was on upside-down.

c) The cynic in you knows that the software will flatly refuse to recognize you, the gate will remain firmly shut and that it is only a matter of time before smoke starts pouring from the machine and you are ushered away to have your passport checked by a human being.

4. **Your senior bus pass operates from 9.30 am, but one day you try to board a bus at 9.26 am. When the driver refuses to allow you on board without paying the full fare, do you?**

   a) Step back and wait for the next bus.

   b) Accept that you are too early and pay the fare because it is your mistake.

   c) Argue with the driver for four minutes, delaying all the other passengers, until it actually is 9.30 and you can get on for free.

5. **As a driver, do you think cyclists should be . . .?**

   a) Treated with consideration for their personal safety.

   b) Barely tolerated.

   c) Banned from the roads and humanity.

6. **Do you think any form of road rage, however mild, is . . .?**

   a) Inexcusable.

   b) Perhaps understandable in exceptional circumstances.

   c) One of the few remaining pleasures you have in life.

7. Which of these drive you to distraction?

a) Someone driving slowly in the fast lane.

b) Someone who takes up two parking spaces.

c) Tailgaters.

d) Loud drum and bass music emanating from a car with dark tinted windows.

e) Students in white stretch limos.

f) Temporary traffic signals that stay on red for ages and then change to green for all of ten seconds.

g) Road works where nobody is working.

h) Speed cameras.

i) Pedestrians who dawdle across the road at designated crossings.

j) Pedestrians who press the street crossing button, forcing you to stop at the light, but then change their mind.

k) Cyclists who ignore red lights.

l) Passengers who are supposed to be giving you clear directions, but are apparently unable to read a simple map. 'It's left at the junction. No, I mean right. Or is it left? One or the other.'

m) Drivers who don't signal at roundabouts.

n) Big trucks on narrow country lanes.

o) Tractors that pull out directly in front of you on narrow country lanes.

p) Pot holes.

q) Motorcyclists who weave in and out of traffic.

r) Creepers at traffic signals who edge forward inch by inch in their cars until the lights go green.

s) Learner drivers who have failed to master the art of

reversing around a corner – or at least aren't as good at it as you think you are.

t) Being two minutes late checking out of the public car park and therefore having to pay for another two hours.

u) Speed bumps.

v) Backseat drivers.

w) Taxi drivers who insist on striking up a conversation requiring sparkling, witty repartee when it's late at night and you are tired and just want to get home.

x) A stranger who thinks your empty driveway gives him the right to use it for his three-point turn.

y) A flat tyre.

z) Anyone in a car that is bigger, newer, cleaner and more expensive than yours.

8. What is your chief topic of conversation while driving long distance?

a) The countryside.

b) Your destination.

c) The state of the roads.

d) Other people's driving.

9. You find a stranger sitting in your reserved seat on the train. Are you more likely to?

a) Say nothing and go and sit in another unoccupied seat if one is available.

b) Show them your reservation and ask them politely to move.

c) Cause a scene.

10. Have you ever taken issue with any passenger who has boarded a train at the station before you have had time to get off?

a) No, it's not worth the hassle.

b) Yes, verbally.

c) Yes, physically.

d) Yes, homicidally.

11. When you get into a taxicab, do you issue directions to the driver?

a) No, there is no need. I am confident that he knows the shortest, quickest route from A to B.

b) Yes, before we even set off I tell him precisely which route I want him to take because the last time I travelled by taxi, I thought the driver was taking me via the North Pole in order to bump up the fare.

12. Which of the following have you cried from behind the wheel of your car recently?

a) 'That idiot's driving way too fast!'

b) 'What the hell does he think he's doing?'

c) 'Did this guy learn to drive on bumper cars?'

d) 'Why is there never a cop car around when you need one?'

e) 'How did that guy ever pass his test?'

f) 'I don't care if that tractor's overtaken us – I'm comfortable at this speed.'

13. **Do you think it would be a good idea if all bus drivers were equipped with a lion on a leash so that when they ask passengers on a crowded vehicle to 'move along the bus, please' to allow extra people to get on, everyone would be encouraged to move more than an inch?**

14. **If a serious traffic accident blocked the road ahead, would your first thought be?**

    a) 'I hope everybody involved is okay.'

    b) 'This is going to add an hour to my journey.'

15. **The airline company wants to charge you and your partner extra for booking seats that are next to each other. Do you think this is . . .?**

    a) Fair enough.

    b) A bit cheeky.

    c) A total liberty, and yet another example of how budget airlines use underhand tactics to push up the price of our fare. Next they'll be charging us to use the emergency escape chute!

16. **Have you ever had a full-blown argument with your car's sat nav?**

17. **On a crowded train, you see an inconsiderate passenger occupying two seats with their bags and coat. Do you?**

    a) Tut about it, but say nothing and go and stand in another part of the train.

    b) Ask: 'Excuse me, is this seat taken?' and then sit down when they grudgingly remove their bags.

c) Say accusingly: 'Excuse me, have you actually paid for both seats?'

d) Snap: 'Hey, move your stuff! I'm not standing for two hours.'

18. A stranger sits next to you on a train even though the rest of the coach is virtually empty. Do you?

a) Say nothing, hoping that he or she will get off soon.

b) Say pointedly: 'There are plenty of empty seats. They're not reserved.'

c) Fidget and nudge them repeatedly with your elbows in the hope of making them so uncomfortable that they decide to move seats. If that fails, develop a sudden hacking cough.

d) Strike up a conversation about incontinence or serial killers.

19. Do you see your electric mobility scooter as . . .?

a) A vehicle.

b) A weapon.

c) I'm not old or infirm enough to own one.

20. If you do own a mobility scooter, when you are driving it do you see yourself as . . .?

a) A sensible, elderly gentleman.

b) Lewis Hamilton.

c) Dick Dastardly.

21. **Are you one of those people who presses the elevator button over and over again at fifteen second intervals, more to register your growing impatience than in any real hope that your actions will make it arrive any sooner?**

22. **Your partner phones you at home in a panic to say that she can't find her car in a busy supermarket car park. Do you say?**
    a) 'Stay calm, honey. I'll be with you in five minutes.'
    b) 'What do you mean, you can't find it? You must remember where you parked it!'
    c) 'I told you we should have bought a purple car. But, oh no, you insisted on silver – just like the rest of the population.'

23. **Do any of the following send you into full grumpy mode when travelling by airplane?**
    a) Being stuck at the check-in desk behind a family who decide to rearrange the entire contents of their cases because one is over the weight limit.
    b) Taking off your belt at security and watching your trousers fall down.
    c) Finding that buying a bottle of water at the airport costs nearly as much as your ticket.
    d) Being overcome by the scent of cheap perfume because the airport has been designed to make sure that you have to pass through the duty-free shop in order to reach the departure gates.

e) Paying extra for priority boarding, only to find that because the incoming plane is late on arrival, all the passengers are let loose at the same time for a mad dash across the tarmac.

f) Seeing a passenger being allowed to carry as free hand luggage a bag that is quite clearly a few centimetres bigger than the maximum size permitted.

g) Passengers who block the aisle and therefore prevent smooth boarding because they are frantically trying to cram their oversized hand luggage into the overhead compartment.

h) Passengers who blatantly ignore the request not to talk through the flight attendants' safety demonstration. If the plane crashes and everyone on board is killed, they'll be the first to complain!

i) Falling asleep peacefully on the plane, but then being rudely awoken by a loud announcement regarding the offer of an 'unbelievable bargain, duty-free perfume at a price too good to miss.'

j) The passenger in the seat next to you placing his elbows on both armrests, even though one is quite clearly designated for your use.

k) Finding that your seat has an area of legroom more suitable for a three-year-old, forcing you to rest your chin on your knees for the entire journey.

l) The first sight of the in-flight meal that you have paid extra for.

m) Stereo crying babies at opposite ends of the plane.

n) Learning that of 'the extensive choice of sandwiches and baguettes' on the menu, all that remains by the time the refreshment trolley has reached your seat is cheese.

o) Finding that a small glass of warm white wine in a plastic cup costs nearly the same as a full bottle at your local supermarket.

p) Seeing that the in-flight movie features a plane crash.

q) The passenger in the next seat continuing to use his laptop even after the announcement stating that all electronic devices must be switched off in readiness for landing.

r) Discovering that the 'unbelievable bargain, duty-free perfume at a price too good to miss' that you were strongly advised to buy on the journey out because stocks were running low is readily available on the flight back – and cheaper.

s) Spotting someone else attempt to take your case off the airport baggage carousel in the mistaken belief that it is theirs.

t) Finding that yours is the very last case off the airport baggage carousel.

u) Observing that, thanks to the ever-caring airport baggage handlers, your previously pristine case now looks as if it has been trampled upon and tossed around by a herd of rampaging elephants.

v) Discovering while unpacking that a bottle in your toiletries bag has leaked on the flight so that the head of your toothbrush now tastes of Burberry cologne.

VACATIONS

1. **On vacation you take a once-in-a-lifetime photo of your partner against a spectacular sunset backdrop, unaware that a stranger has spoiled it by wandering into shot while talking on his phone. Do you?**
   a) Post the picture on Facebook anyway.
   b) Post the picture on Facebook so that all your friends can commiserate with you about your bad luck.
   c) Post the picture on Facebook in the hope of identifying the stranger so that you can then send them an abusive message and a lecture about inconsiderate behaviour.

2. **Have you ever got up at six o'clock in the morning while on vacation because you were absolutely determined that nobody was going to beat you to your favourite poolside sun bed for a third day in a row?**

3. **Has being beaten to your favourite sun bed ever spoiled your whole . . .?**
   a) Morning.
   b) Day.
   c) Vacation.

4. **While on vacation in mainland Europe, you discover that there is no English-speaking channel on the TV in your hotel room. Do you?**
    a) Read a book instead.
    b) Petulantly channel hop between a Slovenian game show, a Croatian soap opera with no subtitles, and a programme where two men and a woman could be discussing either the local mayoral elections or the price of fish – all in the hope that you will eventually find something you can vaguely understand.
    c) Complain to the hotel management that you haven't been able to enjoy your weekly episode of *CSI*.

5. **How do you communicate with local people while on vacation in a non-English speaking country?**
    a) By learning a few words and phrases of their native language.
    b) By the international language of mime.
    c) By talking in English VERY LOUDLY and VERY SLOWLY.

6. **Do you think that all foreigners should be forced to speak English?**

7. **You wake up one morning on vacation to find that you have been bitten by mosquitoes in the night. Your partner, lying next to you in bed, is untouched. Do you say?**
    a) 'I'm so glad you haven't been bitten as well.'

b) 'How come the little blighters have only bitten me and not you? It's not fair!'

8. **After a couple of lunchtime beers, you fall asleep on the sun lounger and wake up sunburned. Do you?**
   a) Accept that you have only yourself to blame and play down the acute pain you are in for fear of drawing further attention to your stupidity.
   b) Accept that you have only yourself to blame but milk your suffering for all it is worth in the hope that the sympathy card will trump the stupidity card.
   c) Blame everyone else in the resort for not waking you when they could see you were turning the colour of a lobster.

9. **Have you ever needed to be rescued – sweating and hyperventilating – from the clutches of a deckchair that you were trying to put up at the time?**

10. **Which part of a vacation do you look forward to the most?**
    a) The sightseeing.
    b) Lazing in the sun.
    c) Being waited on in the hotel.
    d) The food and drink.
    e) Posting a negative review on TripAdvisor.

11. **Are you in a bad mood even before getting to the airport simply because the online weather forecast**

suggests that one day of your ten-day stay in the sunny Mediterranean is going to be blighted by rain?

12. **On vacation, you ask a complete stranger whether he would mind using your camera to take a photo of yourself and your partner, but when you look at the picture he has taken, it is out of focus and the top of your head is missing. Do you?**
    a) Thank him anyway for his time and search for a better photographer.
    b) Ask him to have one more try.
    c) Tell him he's a lousy photographer and should be ashamed of his inability to master an item of equipment that even a three-year-old could use.
    d) Refuse to let him leave until he has got it right.

13. **Have you ever wondered why, after collecting you from the airport, taxi drivers invariably ask whether you have been somewhere nice? What do they expect you to say? 'No, I always like to spend two weeks in the worst place possible – it makes the rest of the year seem so much better.'**

14. **Have you considered a camping vacation recently?**
    a) Yes, it's time spent in the fresh air and it's so cheap.
    b) No, at my age I prefer the warmth and comfort of a nice hotel with waiter service.
    c) Definitely not. Why would you want to spend two weeks sleeping in a muddy field with insects crawling all over

you and a half-mile walk to the nearest toilet in the pitch black of night? It's as much as I can do to make it across the landing at home. My bladder would explode!

15. **If your hotel restaurant has a rule that requires gentlemen to dress smartly for dinner, are you mightily peeved when male guests turn up in swimming shorts and beachwear and none of the staff bat an eyelid?**

16. **When the hotel sports and entertainments officer tours the poolside area looking for volunteers to play water polo or some other water-based activity, do you?**
a) Happily agree to take part.
b) Pretend to be sound asleep.
c) Hide behind a bush until he has gone.

17. Which of the following have you ever complained about to an overseas hotel?

a) The street signs were not in English.

b) You were kept awake at night by your partner's snoring.

c) The framed print in your room was not to your artistic taste.

d) The sea was too cold.

e) The sea was too noisy.

f) The beach was too sandy and it kept getting between your toes.

g) The sand was too hot to walk on.

h) The sand on the beach was whiter than in the brochure.

i) The local store did not sell your favourite brand of chocolate bar.

j) The weather was so hot that the ice in your drink kept melting too quickly.

k) The Elvis tribute act that constituted the hotel entertainment one night wasn't really Elvis at all, but a plumber from Valencia.

l) You were bitten by a mosquito even though the hotel brochure made no mention of mosquitoes.

m) You bought a pair of 'authentic Ray-Ban sunglasses' for five dollars from a street trader, only to find they were fake.

n) The tide was in sometimes.

o) You thought the drinks in the room minibar were complimentary.

p) The waiter was too handsome, so your partner spent the whole fortnight looking at him instead of you.

q) There was no roast beef on Sundays in the hotel restaurant – and you always have roast beef on a Sunday at home.

r) The shower cap wasn't your size.

s) You kept forgetting the combination that you had keyed in to the room safe.

t) All of the English newspapers were a day late.

u) The resort was full of foreigners.

v) The receptionist kept hiding when you arrived at the desk with a new grievance.

18. How many days into a seven-day vacation do you start fussing about the journey home?

a) Seven.

b) Six.

c) One.

WEATHER

1. **It rains all morning on a summer's day. Do you think?**
   a) 'Never mind, it's good for the garden.'
   b) 'It will probably ease off soon.'
   c) 'I'm damn sure it never used to rain in June back in the 1950s.'

2. **Which of the following makes you grumpy?**
   a) Extremely hot weather.
   b) Extremely cold weather.
   c) Extremely wet weather.
   d) Extremely windy weather.
   e) A cloudy day without a hint of sun.
   f) Fog.
   g) Scattered showers that all fall on you.
   h) An inaccurate weather forecast.

3. **Even on a bright, sunny day with no rain forecast, do you still pick up your umbrella when you leave the house – just in case?**

4. **The sun inconsiderately shines on the TV screen in your lounge, making it difficult for you to see the picture. Do you think?**

a) 'Who cares about the TV show? It's so nice to see the sun for a change.'

b) 'Typical! It's cloudy all day and then the moment I want to watch something, the sun comes out and spoils my pleasure. It's never liked me.'

5. **You read that long-range weather forecasters are predicting the harshest winter for fifty years. Do you?**

a) Rush out to buy a thicker duvet and a new pair of gloves, get the central heating boiler serviced in readiness, bring the snow shovel in from the shed, buy a back-up generator, and stock up on emergency supplies of canned food – including every available can of tomato soup within a twenty-mile radius – in case you are unable to leave your home for weeks.

b) Wait and see.

c) Scoff: 'That's what they say every year – and they haven't been right once. How can they predict the weather three months ahead when they can't even tell you whether or not it's going to be raining tomorrow? To my mind, the only way to get an accurate weather forecast is to look out of the window!'

6. **Do you find it irritating when the people who say after a heavy snowfall, 'Doesn't it look pretty?' are always the ones who don't have to travel anywhere for the next few days?**

7. **When people complain about a few flakes of snow, do you hear yourself saying?**
   a) 'Yes, it's a nuisance, isn't it?'
   b) 'Don't worry, I'm sure with global warming it will soon melt.'
   c) 'You can't call that snow! It's barely a covering. I've seen heavier falls of dandruff! I'll show you pictures of what real snow looks like. In my day, we had *proper* winters!'

8. **On a wet and windy day, is anything more likely to tip you over the edge than your umbrella blowing inside out? Not only does it lead to you getting soaked, it is acutely embarrassing as you try in vain to correct it. You feel that all eyes on the busy street are trained on you, laughing at your abject humiliation, with everyone thinking: 'What an idiot! What a cheap umbrella!' Your only consolation is the knowledge that the umbrella is now living on borrowed time. If it shows you up again in public, it's going straight in the bin.**

9. **Which of these weather conditions would best describe you?**
   a) Sunny.
   b) Dull and overcast.

c) Cold and frosty.

d) Occasionally stormy.

e) Windy.

10. **Are you firmly convinced that all of today's extreme climatic conditions stem from the Russians sending Yuri Gagarin into space back in 1961?**

11. **You learn that the weather back home is much better than the weather you are experiencing on vacation. Do you?**

a) Conclude that it's just the luck of the draw and continue enjoying your holiday as best as you can.

b) Fret constantly over the weather back home, going online for regular updates, phoning neighbours and not resting until you are absolutely satisfied that rain is falling on your house.

WORK

1. **In the office, you are asked to fetch the morning cups of tea two days in a row. Do you say?**

   a) 'That's okay. The walk will do me good.'

   b) 'It must be someone else's turn. I did the tea run yesterday.'

   c) 'We really need to draw up an enforceable rota for this.'

2. **You are asked to attend the leaving party of someone you have never liked. Do you?**

   a) Bury the hatchet and let bygones be bygones.

   b) Say nice things about them through gritted teeth.

   c) Take the day off sick.

3. **On a scale of zero (relaxed indifference) to ten (incandescent with rage), how irritated do you get if your company-supplied, free ballpoint pen vanishes inexplicably from your work desk?**

4. **A newcomer to the firm takes your favourite coffee mug, even though you have written your name on it in large letters. Do you say?**

   a) 'Sorry, that one's mine. I should have said. Would you mind using another mug, please?'

b) 'What's the matter? Can't you read?'

c) 'Try that again and I'll report you to HR.'

5. **Is your only concession to 'dress-down Friday' at work to loosen the knot in your necktie a little?**

6. **Do your work colleagues often refer to you as . . .?**

   a) Jolly George (or whatever your name is).

   b) Good old George.

   c) George.

   d) The miserable old bastard in the corner.

7. **Do work colleagues snigger because you still think the best way to resolve a dispute is to pick up the phone and have a proper, grown-up conversation rather than send an email which could easily be misinterpreted, get lost somewhere in cyberspace or go to the wrong person altogether because you have not yet got the hang of sending emails?**

8. **Which of these occupations could society happily exist without?**

   a) Personal injury lawyers.

   b) Bankers.

   c) Jugglers.

   d) Social workers.

   e) Circus clowns.

   f) Politicians.

   g) Sports commentators.

   h) Public relations executives.

   i) Children's entertainers.

   j) Child singers.

   k) Tabloid journalists.

   l) Performance artists.

   m) Management consultants.

   n) Parking enforcement officers (traffic wardens in old money).

   o) Tap dancers.

   p) Insurance salesmen.

   q) Daytime TV presenters.

   r) Pet psychics.

9. **What do you think is the principal objective of an office meeting?**

   a) To communicate information and ideas.

   b) To kill time between lunch and five-thirty.

   c) To make a few middle management nonentities look important.

10. **Have you ever walked out of a meeting because everyone else present is using corporate speak and you can't understand a word they are saying?**

11. **Have you ever been tempted to take an axe to a superior at work who dismisses your valid point with the words: 'I hear what you say'?**

12. **Do you think that there is only ever justification for using the phrase 'pushing the envelope' at work if you work for the post office?**

13. **You are asked to contribute towards the leaving gift for a work colleague whom you barely know. Do you?**
    a) Put a few coins of small denomination into the envelope so as not to appear mean.
    b) Say, 'Sorry, I don't know her,' and walk off.
    c) Say, 'Sorry, I don't have any cash on me today,' and hope that the collector either forgets to ask you again or is unable to find you. This may require suddenly dashing to the toilet and hiding there to avoid the aforementioned collector or, in extreme circumstances, wearing sunglasses and a false beard for the rest of the week.

14. **Which of these workplace truisms do you agree with?**
    a) The longer the job title, the less important the job.
    b) A consultant is a man who knows one hundred and seventeen ways to make love, but doesn't know any women.

c) Blessed are those who have nothing to say and who cannot be persuaded to say it.

d) When bosses talk about improving productivity, they are never talking about themselves.

e) Teamwork means never having to take all the blame.

f) People who can, work all day; people who can't, sit in meetings all day.

g) As soon as you get a cup of coffee, your boss will assign you a task that lasts just long enough for your coffee to go cold.

h) There is no limit to the progress you can make within a company if you always look serious and carry a clipboard.

i) It is important to get right behind your boss because that's the only way you can stab him in the back.

j) If an over-confident work colleague boasts that he is doing the job of two men, you can bet that the two men in question are Abbott and Costello.

k) People who go to conferences are the ones who shouldn't.

l) If you can smile when everything around you is going wrong, you're probably in the repair business.

15. **Have you ever launched a full-scale, internal investigation after a person or persons unknown altered the height of your office chair?**

YOUNG PEOPLE

1. **Which of the following do you think would be beneficial to the youngsters of today?**

   a) A good education.

   b) Positive role models within the family.

   c) Compulsory military service.

   d) A week in the stocks.

2. **Do you believe that the only instance when it is acceptable to use the phrase 'check out this bad boy' is when referring to a young offender?**

3. **What do you think is a suitable reward for a trick or treater at Halloween?**

   a) Some candy.

   b) A pack of stale cookies that are three years past their expiry date.

   c) A shake of the fist and a warning never to darken this door again.

4. **Do you tend to correct a young person if they use the phrase 'should of' in conversation?**

5. **Do you find young people with facial piercings to be . . .?**

   a) Refreshingly free-spirited.

   b) Perfectly normal.

   c) Mildly disconcerting.

   d) Downright scary.

6. **There are no empty seats on a crowded bus, but because you are tired and need to rest your legs, you deliberately stand next to a young person in the hope that they will get up and offer you their seat. Is your chosen tactic?**

   a) To mop your brow and generally look old and frail so that they might take pity on you.

   b) To glare at them, defying them to remain seated.

   c) To grab your chest dramatically, feigning an impending heart attack.

d) To 'accidentally' tread on their toes a couple of times until they realize it will be less painful to let you have the seat.

e) To gripe loudly to the rest of the bus about 'the youth of today', lobbing in references to 'elders and betters', 'sacrifices' and 'El Alamein', even though you were born twelve years after the end of World War II.

7. **A young person tries to 'high-five' you. Do you?**
    a) Attempt to 'high-five' him back, and hope that nobody is watching in case you miss.
    b) Back away, saying: 'Sorry, I don't do that sort of thing.'
    c) Misinterpret his raised hand as an attempted assault, and call the police.

8. **When it comes to careers, do you prefer to hear that friends' children are?**
    a) Doing well.
    b) Doing quite well but not as well as your children.
    c) Failing miserably.

9. **Do you get annoyed by student protests – but solely because you know that the only sit-in you are likely to be involved in these days is the result of constipation?**

10. Which of these is likely to get your hackles up?

a) A young person with their feet up on the opposite seat on public transport.

b) A young person telling you to 'take a chill pill'.

c) A young person whose conversation is peppered with phrases such as 'so random', 'from the get-go', and 'no brainer'.

d) A young person who inserts 'like' between every other word.

e) A young person who adds 'hashtag something' to the end of a spoken sentence. What's that all about?

f) A young person calling you 'grandad' when he or she is not a relative.

g) A young person calling you 'grandad' when you have only just turned forty.

11. In general, do you think?

a) It's really tough for young people these days, with a shortage of jobs and affordable housing.

b) Young people don't know how lucky they are, compared with what we had to go through when we were their age. They've never had to walk eight miles to work and back again each day in shoes with soles no thicker than a slice of wafer-thin ham; they've never had to endure a proper winter with six feet of snow for weeks on end, before all this modern fancy climate change; they've never had to make their own entertainment by watching the rising damp creep up the walls of their bedroom; they've never had to wear their elder sibling's hand-me-downs, which is really embarrassing when you're the only boy in class wearing a floral dress; they've never had to lose the TV picture at the crucial point in a western just because the woman next door decided to switch on her hoover; they've never had to sit at the tap end of the bathtub; they've never had to eat bread and fish paste for tea six nights a week – and be grateful for it; they've never had to suffer as their dentist bored into their teeth with an implement the size of a road drill; and don't get me going on daily doses of cod liver oil . . .

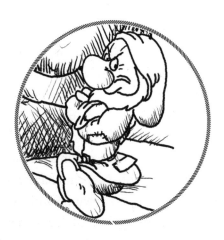

ANSWERS

Now, to test your grumpy old git rating, add up your scores — if it's not too much trouble.

ACCIDENTS

1. a)0 b)1 c)2
2. a)1 b)2 c)3
3. a)0 b)1 c)2 d)3
4. no)0, yes)2
5. a)0 b)1 c)2
6. a)0 b)2

7. no)0 yes)2
8. a)0 b)2
9. a)0 b)1 c)2
10. a)1 b)2
11. a,b,c,d)0 e) 2

ANIMALS

1. a)0 b)1 c)2
2. a,b)0 c)2
3. a)0 b)2
4. no)0 yes)2
5. a)0 b)1 c)2
6. a,b)0 c)2
7. a)0 b)1 c)2
8. a,b)0 c)2

9. a)0 b)2
10. a)0 b)1
11. a,b)0 c)2
12. a)0 b)2
13. a,b)0 c)1 d)2
14. a)0 b)1 c,d)2
15. no)0 yes)2
16. a,b)0 c)1 d,e)2

BEHAVIOUR

1. 2 for each answer
2. a,b)0 c)2
3. no)0 yes)2
4. a,b)0 c)1
5. no)0 yes)2
6. a,b)0 c)1
7. no)0 yes)2
8. a)1 b)2 c)3 d)4
9. no)0 yes)2
10. a,b)0 c)3
11. no)0 yes)1
12. a,b)0 c)2
13. no)0 yes)2
14. a)1 b)2 c,d,e,f,g)3
15. no)0 yes)2
16. a)0 b)1 c)2 d)3
17. no)0 yes)1
18. a)0 b)1 c)2
19. no)0 yes)2
20. a)0 b)1 c)2 d)3 e)4
21. no)0 yes)2
22. a,b,c)2 d)0 e,f,g)2 h)0 i)2
    j)5
23. a)0 b)2
24. no)0 yes)2
25. no)0 yes)2
26. no)0 yes)2
27. 2 for each answer

BOOKS

1. a)0 b)1 c)2
2. a,b,c,d)1 e,f)2
3. no)0 yes)2
4. a)0 b)1 c)2
5. no)0 yes)2
6. a)0 b)1 c)2
7. a)0 b)2
8. no)0 yes)2
9. a)0 b)1 c)2.
10. no)0 yes)2

CHRISTMAS

1. a,b.c.d)0 e)2
2. a)0 b)1 c)2
3. a)0 b)1 c)2
4. a)0 b,c)1 d)2
5. a)0 b)2
6. no)0 yes)2
7. 2 for each answer
8. no)0 yes)2
9. a)0 b,c)2
10. no)0 yes)1
11. no)0 yes)1
12. a)0 b)2
13. a)0 b)1 c)2
14. no)0 yes)2
15. a)0 b)2
16. a)1 b)2 c)3
17. a)0 2 for each of the remaining answers
18. a)0 b)1 c)2
19. a)0 b)2
20. a)0 b,c)2
21. 1 for each answer

CLOTHES

1. a,b)0 c)2
2. a)0 b)1 c)2
3. a)1 b)2 c)3 d)4
4. a)0 b)1 c)2
5. no)0 yes)1
6. a)0 b)1 c)2
7. no)0 yes)2
8. a)0 b)2
9. a,b)0 c)2
10. no)0 yes)2
11. no)0 yes)2
12. a)0 b)2
13. no)0 yes)2
14. no)0 yes)2
15. a,b)0 c)2

COMMUNICATION

1. a)4 b)3 c)2 d)1
2. a)0 b)1 c)2
3. a)0 b)2
4. a)0 b)2
5. a)0 b)1 c)2 d)4
6. a)2 b)0 c)1
7. a)0 b)1 c)2
8. a)0 b)1 c)2
9. no)0 yes)2
10. a)0 b)1
11. a)0 b)2
12. a)0 b,c)2
13. a)0 b)2
14. no)0 yes)2
15. a)0 b)1 c)2
16. a,b)0 c)2
17. no)0 yes)2
18. a)0 b)1 c)2
19. no)0 yes)2
20. a)0 b,c)2
21. no)0 yes)2
22. a)0 b)2
23. no)0 yes)2
24. a,b)0 c)1 d)2
25. a)0 b)1 c)2

EDUCATION

1. 2 for each 'yes' answer
2. a,b)0 c)2
3. a)0 b)2
4. a,c)0 b)2
5. a)0 b)1 c)2

FAMILY

1. a)0 b)1 c)2
2. no)0 yes)2
3. a)0 b)1 c)2
4. a)0 b)1 c)2
5. a)0 b)1 c)2
6. a)0 b,c)2
7. no)0 yes)2
8. a)0 b)1 c)2
9. no)0 yes)2
10. a)5 b)2 c)0 d)1 e)0 f)0 g)0 h)0
11. a)0 b)1 c)2
12. 2 for each answer
13. a)0 b)2 c)3
14. 2 for each answer

FOOD AND DRINK

1. a)0 b)1 c)2
2. a)0 b,c)2
3. a)0 b,c)2
4. a)0 b)1 c)2
5. no)0 yes)2
6. a)0 b)2
7. no)0 yes)2
8. a,b,c)0 d)2
9. a)0 b,c)1
10. 2 for each answer
11. a)0 b)1 c)2 d)3
12. a)0 b)1 c)2 d)0
13. no)0 yes)2
14. a)0 b)2
15. no)0 yes)2
16. a)0 b)1 c)2
17. no)0 yes)2
18. a,b)0 c)2
19. no)0 yes)2
20. a)0 b,c)2 d)1
21. no)0 yes)2
22. a)0 b)2
23. 2 for each answer
24. a)0 b,c)2

GARDENING

1. a)0 b)2 c)3
2. a)0 b)1 c)2 d)3
3. no)0 yes)2
4. a)0 b)1 c)2
5. no)0 yes)2
6. a)0 b)1 c)2 d)3
7. no)0 yes)2
8. 2 for each 'yes' answer
9. no)0 yes)2
10. a)0 b)1 c)2
11. 2 for each 'yes' answer

THE GOOD OLD DAYS

1. no)0 yes) 2
2. a)0 b)2
3. 2 for each answer
4. no)0 yes)2
5. no)0 yes) 2
6. no)0 yes)2
7. no)0 yes)2

HEALTH

1. 2 for each answer
2. a)2 b)0
3. a,b)0 c)2
4. a)0 b)2
5. no)0 yes)2
6. a,b)2 c)3
7. a)0 b)1 c)2
8. a)2 b)1 c)2 d)2 e)1
9. no)0 yes)2
10. a)0 b)1 c)2
11. no)0 yes)2
12. a,b)0 c)2
13. a)0 b)2
14. no)0 yes)2
15. a)0 b)1 c)2
16. a,b)0 c)3
17. a)0 b)2
18. no)0 yes)2
19. yes)0 no)2
20. a,b,c)0 2 for each of the remaining answers

HOBBIES AND RECREATION

1. a)0 b)1 c,d)2
2. a,b)0 c)2
3. no)0 yes)2
4. a)0 b)2
5. a)2 b)1 c)0
6. a,b)0 c)1 d)2
7. no)0 yes)2
8. a,b)0 c)2
9. no)0 yes)2
10. a)0 b)1 c)2
11. a)0 b)2
12. no)0 yes)2
13. a)0 b,c)2
14. no)0 yes)2
15. a)0 b,c)2

THE HOME

1. a)0 b)1 c)2	12. a)0 b)1 c)2 d)3
2. 2 points for each 'yes' answer	13. no)0 yes)2
	14. a)1 b)2
3. a)0 b)1 c)2	15. a)0 b)2
4. no)0 yes)2	16. no)0 yes)2
5. no)0 yes)2	17. a)0 b)1 c)2
6. a)0 b)1 c)2	18. a)0 b)1 c)2
7. a)0 b)2	19. no)0 yes)2
8. a)0 b)1 c)2	20. a)0 b)1 c)2 d)3 e)4
9. a)0 b.c)2	21. no)0 yes)2
10. no)0 yes)2	22. no)0 yes) 2
11. a)0 b)1 c)2	23. a,b)0 c)2

LAW AND ORDER

1. a)0 b)1 c)2	5. no)0 yes)2
2. 2 for each answer	6. a)0 b)1 c)2
3. no)0 yes)2	7. no)0 yes)2
4. a,b)0 c)2	8. 2 for each 'yes' answer

MONEY

1. a)0 b,c)2	7. no)0 yes)2
2. no)0 yes)2	8. a)0 b,c)2
3. a)0 b)1 c)2	9. no)0 yes)2
4. a)0 b)1 c)2 d)3	10. a)0 b)1 c)2
5. no)0 yes)2	11. no)0 yes)2
6. a)0 b)1 c)2	12 no)0 yes)2

MOVIES

1. a)0 b)2
2. a)0 b)1 c)2 d)3
3. a)0 b)1 c)2
4. no)0 yes)2
5. no)0 yes)2
6. a)0 b)2
7. a,b)0 c)2
8. no)0 yes)2
9. no)0 yes)2

MUSIC

1. a)0 b)1 c)2
2. yes)0 no)2
3. a)0 b)2
4. no)0 yes)2
5. 2 for each 'yes' answer
6. no)0 yes)2
7. a,b)0 c)1 d)2
8. no)0 yes)2
9. a,b)1 c)2
10. no)0 yes)2
11. minus 1 for each answer a-j, plus 2 for k
12. no)0 yes)2
13. no)0 yes)2
14. a)0 b)2
15. no)0 yes)2
16. a,b)1 c,d)2
17. yes)1 no)2

POLITICS

1. a)0 b)1 c)2
2. a)0 b)1 c)2
3. a,b)1 c)2
4. a)0 b)1 c)2
5. a)0 b)1 c)2
6. a)0 b)1 c)2
7. a)0 b)1 c)2
8. a,b,c)0 d)2
9. a)0 b)1 c)2
10. a)0 b,c)2
11. a,b)0 c)2

RELATIONSHIPS

1. a)1 b)2 c)3
2. a,b)0 c)2
3. a)0 b)1 c)2
4. a,b)0 c)1 d)2
5. a)3 b)2 c)1
6. a)0 b)1 c)2 d)3
7. a)0 b)1 c)2

8. a)0 b)1 c)2
9. 2 for each 'yes' answer
10. a,b)0 c,d)2 e)3
11. no)0 yes)2
12. a)0 b)1 c)2
13. 2 for each 'yes' answer

SERVICES

1. a)0 b)1 c)2 d)3
2. a,b)0 c)2
3. a)0 b,c)2
4. no)0 yes)2
5. yes)0 no)2
6. no)0 yes)2
7. no)0 yes)2

8. a)0 b)2
9. no)0 yes)2
10. a)1 b)2 c)3
11. no)0 yes)2
12. a)0 b)2
13. no)0 yes)2
14. 2 for each answer

SHOPPING

1. a)0 b)1 c)2
2. a)2 b)1 c)0
3. a)0 b)2
4. a)2 b)1 c)0
5. no)0 yes)2
6. a)0 b)1 c)2
7. no)0 yes)2
8. a)0 b)1 c)2

9. a)0 b)2
10. no)0 yes)2
11. a)0 b)1 c)2 d)3
12. no)0 yes)2
13. 2 for each answer
14. no)0 yes)2
15. 2 for each answer

SPORTS

1. a)0 b)1 c)2
2. a)0 b)1 c)2 d)3
3. no)0 yes)2
4. a,b)0 c)2
5. no)0 yes)2
6. a)0 b)2
7. no)0 yes)2
8. a)0 b)1 c)2
9. no)0 yes)2
10. a)0 b)1 c)2 d)3

11. a,b)1 c)2
12. no)0 yes)2
13. a,b)0 c)2
14. no)0 yes)2
15. a)0 b)2
16. no)0 yes)2
17. 2 for each answer
18. no)0 yes)2
19. a)0 b)1 c)2

TECHNOLOGY

1. a,b)0 c)2 d)3
2. a,b)0 c)2
3. no)0 yes)2
4. 2 for each 'yes' answer
5. no)0 yes)2
6. no)0 yes)2
7. 2 for each answer
8. no)0 yes)2
9. no)0 yes)2
10. a,b,d,e)1 c)0

11. no)0 yes)2
12. no)0 yes)2
13. no)0 yes)2
14. no)0 yes)2
15. yes)0 no)2
16. a,b)0 c)2
17. no)0 yes)2
18. no)0 yes)2
19. no)0 yes)2
20. a-h)1 for each answer i)4

TELEVISION

1. a,b)0 c)1 d)2
2. a)0 b)1 c)2
3. a)0 b)1 c)2
4. a)0 b)1 c)2
5. no)1 yes)2
6. no)0 yes)2
7. a,b)0 c)2
8. no)0 yes)2
9. a,b)0 c)2
10. no)0 yes)2
11. 2 for each answer
12. no)0 yes)2
13. a)0 b)1 c)2
14. no)0 yes)2
15. no)0 yes)2
16. a)0 b)1 c)2

TRAVEL

1. a,b)0 c)2
2. a)0 b)1 c)2
3. a)0 b)1 c)2
4. a,b)0 c)2
5. a)0 b)1 c)2
6. a)0 b)1 c)2
7. 2 for each answer
8. a,b)0 c)2 d)3
9. a,b)0 c)2
10. a)0 b)1 c)2 d)5
11. a)0 b)2
12. 2 for each answer
13. no)0 yes)2
14. a)0 b)2
15. a)0 b)1 c)2
16. no)0 yes)2
17. a)1 b)2 c)3 d)4
18. a)1 b)2 c)3 d)1
19. a)0 b)2 c)3
20. a)0 b)1 c)2
21. no)0 yes)2
22. a)0 b,c)2
23. 2 for each 'yes' answer

VACATIONS

1. a,b)0 c)2
2. no)0 yes)2
3. a)1 b)2 c)3
4. a)0 b)1 c)2
5. a)0 b)1 c)2
6. no)0 yes)2
7. a)0 b)2
8. a)0 b)1 c)2
9. no)0 yes)2
10. a,b,c,d)0 e)2
11. no)0 yes)2
12. a)0 b)1 c)2 d)3
13. no)0 yes)2
14. a)0 b)1 c)2
15. no)0 yes)2
16. a)0 b)1 c)2
17. 2 for each answer
18. a)0 b)1 c)2

WEATHER

1. a,b)0 c)2
2. 2 for each answer
3. no)0 yes)2
4. a)0 b)2
5. a)1 b)0 c)2
6. no)0 yes)2
7. a,b)0 c)2
8. yes)0 no)2
9. a)0 b)1 c,d)2 e)1
10. no)0 yes)2
11. a)0 b)2

WORK

1. a)0 b)1 c)2
2. a)0 b)1 c)2
3. 0-10 according to score
4. a)0 b)1 c)2
5. no)0 yes)2
6. a,b,c)0 d)2
7. no)0 yes)2
8. 2 for each answer
9. a)0 b)1 c)2
10. no)0 yes)2
11. no)0 yes)2
12. no)0 yes)2
13. a)0 b)1 c)2
14. 2 for each answer
15. no)0 yes)2

YOUNG PEOPLE

1. a,b)0 c)1 d)2
2. no)0 yes)2
3. a)0 b)1 c)2
4. no)0 yes)2
5. a,b)0 c)1 d)2
6. a)1 b)2 c)3 d)4 e)5

7. a)1 b)2 c)3
8. a)0 b)1 c)2
9. no)0 yes)2
10. 2 for each answer
11. a)0 b)5

Check your grumpy scale rating

0–700 points: You're no grumpier than the next man – particularly if the next man happens to be C. Montgomery Burns – but you occasionally become frustrated by life's little trials. It's nothing that a nice warm bath, a slice of chocolate cake and six months of intensive therapy won't cure.

700–1200: It doesn't take much to bring out your inner grump, but people probably love you just the way you are. Or at least they're not brave enough to tell you differently.

1200–1790: You've definitely inherited the grumpy gene. But remember, if everyone was happy all the time, nothing would ever improve. If early Man hadn't kept complaining about the cold, we might never have had fire; if Alexander Graham Bell hadn't become fed up with writing letters, he would probably never have come up with the idea of the telephone; and if Joseph Gayetty hadn't grumbled about finding the financial pages of *The New York Times* imprinted on his backside, he would never have invented toilet paper. The world needs its share of grumpy old gits.